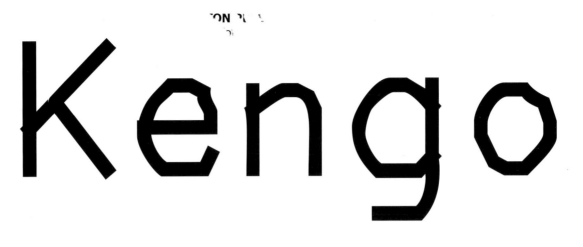

Kengo

Breathing Architecture

Kuma

The Teahouse of the Museum of Applied Arts Frankfurt

Das Teehaus des Museums für Angewandte Kunst Frankfurt

Volker Fischer / Ulrich Schneider (Eds.)

Birkhäuser

Basel · Boston · Berlin

Edited and published by the Museum of Applied Arts Frankfurt

Commissioned by Dezernat für Kultur und Wissenschaft Frankfurt am Main

Translation from German into English: Elizabeth Schwaiger, Toronto

Translation from Japanese into German of essays by Kuma and Saikawa: Wolfgang Höhn and Mariko Sakai, Frankfurt am Main

Translation from Japanese into English of Kuma essay: Gary Dyck, Tōkyō / Editing: Monica Buckland, Basel

Translation from Japanese into English of Saikawa essay: Gary Dyck, Tōkyō / Editing: Elizabeth Schwaiger, Toronto

Editing: Volker Fischer, Thomas Menzel

Design: VIER5, Paris

Library of Congress Control Number: 2008922776

Bibliographic information published by the German National Library

The German National Library lists this publication in the Deutsche Nationalbibliografie; detailed bibliographic data are available on the Internet at http://dnb.d-nb.de.

Published by Birkhäuser Verlag AG
Basel · Boston · Berlin

P.O. Box 133, CH-4010 Basel, Switzerland
Part of Springer Science+Business Media

Printed on acid-free paper produced from chlorine-free pulp. TCF ∞

ISBN: 978-3-7643-8787-7

9 8 7 6 5 4 3 2 1

www.birkhauser.ch

Greetings

In his teahouse for the Museum of Applied Arts Frankfurt, the architect Kengo Kuma has created a work that exemplifies the fundamental pillars of Japanese culture: tradition and innovation. While the exterior of this air-supported building displays as futuristic structure, the interior adheres to design principles that were developed in the sixteenth century under Sen no Rikyū (1522-1591). The teahouse is thus a natural complement to the Japanese collection of the museum, but it is also a symbol of the close links between Japan and Germany, Hessen and Frankfurt am Main. In the anticipation that this teahouse will make an important contribution to strengthening the relationships between Germany and Japan, I extend my wishes for success to the teahouse and the Museum of Applied Arts Frankfurt and many meditative tea ceremonies.

I would also like to take this opportunity to express my heartfelt thanks to all individuals and companies who have contributed to the successful realization of the Teahouse Project.

Yoshitaka Hanada, Consul General of Japan in Frankfurt am Main

Grußwort

Mit seinem Teehaus für das Museum für Angewandte Kunst Frankfurt hat der Architekt Kengo Kuma ein Werk geschaffen, das die Grundpfeiler japanischer Kultur beispielhaft vorführt: Tradition und Innovation. Zeigt das Äußere dieses luftgestützten Gebäudes eine futuristische Struktur, so folgt dessen Einrichtung den Gestaltungsprinzipien, wie sie sich im 16. Jahrhundert unter Sen no Rikyū (1522-1591) entwickelten. So fügt sich das Teehaus wohl zur japanischen Kunstsammlung des Museums. Es ist aber auch Zeichen der engen Verbundenheit Japans mit Deutschland, Hessen und Frankfurt am Main. In der Erwartung, dass dieses Teehaus einen bedeutenden Beitrag zur Stärkung der deutsch-japanischen Beziehungen leisten wird, wünsche ich dem Teehaus und dem Museum für Angewandte Kunst Frankfurt viel Erfolg und viele meditative Teezeremonien. Ich möchte diese Gelegenheit auch wahrnehmen, all den Menschen und den Firmen, die zum Gelingen des Teehaus-Projektes beigetragen haben, meinen ganz herzlichen Dank auszusprechen.

Yoshitaka Hanada, Japanischer Generalkonsul in Frankfurt am Main

Kengo Kuma & Associates

Teahouse July 2005-August 2007
Teehaus Juli 2005-August 2007

Museum of Applied Arts, Frankfurt
Museum für Angewandte Kunst Frankfurt

The organization committee
Das Organisationskomitee

Kōichi Nezu
Kunio Kuroda
Nobutada Saji
Sōichirō Fukutake
Yōichirō Ushioda
Yoshiharu Fukuhara
Yūzaburō Mogi

We are indebted to the following businesses for
making the realization of the Teahouse Project
for the Museum of Applied Arts Frankfurt possible/
Die Verwirklichung des Teehaus-Projektes für
das Museum für Angewandte Kunst Frankfurt ist
folgenden Unternehmen zu verdanken:

ABC Trading Co., Ltd.
Asahi Woodtec Corporation
Asano Fire-Retardant Lumber Co., Ltd.
Cassina IXC Ltd.
Central Glass Co., Ltd.
Clifford Chance
Daikō Electric Co., Ltd.
Device, Inc.
W.L. Gore & Associates
Hasekō Corporation
Ishikawajima Transport Machinery Co., Ltd.
Japan Airlines
Japan Foundation
Japanisches Generalkonsulat Frankfurt
am Main
Kajima Corporation
Kawashima Selkon Textiles Co., Ltd.
Kinden Corporation
Kokuyo Furniture Co., Ltd.
Kokuyo Office System Co., Ltd.
Konoike Construction Co., Ltd.
Maeda Corporation
Max Kenzō Roofing
Matsushita Electric Works, Ltd.
Messe Frankfurt Exhibition GmbH
B. Metzler seel. Sohn und Co. KGaA
Nichibei Co., Ltd.
Nomura Co., Ltd.
Nozawa Corporation
Ōbayashi Corporation
Okamura Corporation
Sankyō Tateyama Aluminium Inc.
Sanwa Shutter Corporation
Shimizu Corporation
Suntory Limited
SUS Corporation
Taisei Corporation
Taiyō Europe GmbH
Tajima Roofing Inc.
Takenaka Corporation
Techno Namiken Co., Ltd.
Tonets Corporation
Tostem Corporation
TRUMPF GmbH + Co. KG
YKK AP Inc.

The working committee/Das Arbeitskomitee

Design/Gesamtplanung:
Kengo Kuma & Associates, J-Tōkyō
Kengo Kuma, Takumi Saikawa, Katinka Temme

Membrane design/Planung Membran:
Hidenari Matsumoto, Taiyo Europe GmbH, D-München
Gerd Schmid, formTL ingenieure für tragwerk und
leichtbau gmbH, D-Radolfzell

Shell work execution/Ausführung Rohbau:
Takenaka Europe GmbH, D-Düsseldorf

Membrane execution/Ausführung Membran:
Canobbio S.p.A., I-Castelnuovo Scrivia

Compressed air blower/Ausführung Luftdruck-
gebläse: Gustav Nolting GmbH, D-Detmold

Compressed air ducts/Ausführung Druckluftleitung:
Fredi Spahn, D-Frankfurt am Main

Electric installation/Ausführung Elektroinstallationen:
H. Müller GmbH, D-Frankfurt am Main

Civil engineering/Ausführung Tiefbau:
Ackermann GmbH, D-Frankfurt am Main

Lighting/Beleuchtung:
Matsushita Electric Works, Ltd., J-Tōkyō/Ōsaka
Panasonic Electric Works Vossloh-Schwabe GmbH,
D-Lüdenscheid

Curators/Kuratoren

Prof. Dr. Ulrich Schneider, Dr. Stephan Graf von
der Schulenburg, Museum für Angewandte Kunst
Frankfurt
Miki Shimokawa, D-Frankfurt am Main/J-Kyōto
Maria-Isabel Martín-Peláez, Peter Maurer,
Hochbauamt der Stadt Frankfurt am Main
Gabriele Schuster, Kulturamt der Stadt Frankfurt
am Main

Foreword

Since the summer of 2007, the Museum of Applied Arts in Frankfurt is home to a very unique Japanese teahouse.
The Japanese architect Kengo Kuma conceived this highly innovative building as an inflatable structure for rapid and easy installation and disassembly.
This publication describes the genesis, the technology and the role of the teahouse in the context of traditional Japanese and modern international architecture; it is also a profile of this project as a product of an international collaboration that continues to this day. Last but not least, the teahouse also symbolizes the long-standing close connection between the Museum of Applied Arts in Frankfurt and Japanese culture.
Many individuals, companies and institutions have contributed to the realization of the building. It is thanks to their dedication that we are in possession today of a valuable art object of Breathing Architecture. We thank all of them in the table of appreciation on the facing page. To Kengo Kuma and his associates, we express our gratitude for a wonderful idea and their friendship.
We would also like to extend our thanks to Birkhäuser Verlag, Basel, Berlin, Boston for the dedicated, always reliable and professional collaboration.

Prof. Dr. Ulrich Schneider, Director,
Museum of Applied Arts Frankfurt

Prof. Dr. Volker Fischer, Curator of Design
at the Museum of Applied Arts Frankfurt

Dr. Stephan Graf v. d. Schulenburg, Curator for Art from the Middle East, East Asia and Southeast Asia at the Museum of Applied Arts Frankfurt

Vorwort

Seit Sommer 2007 ist das Museum für Angewandte Kunst Frankfurt Eigentümer eines japanischen Teehauses ganz besonderer Art. Der japanische Architekt Kengo Kuma hat diesen hoch innovativen Bau als aufblasbare, schnell installierbare und demontierbare Struktur konzipiert.
Die vorliegende Publikation beschreibt das Entstehen, die Technik und die Aufgabe des Teehauses in Verbindung mit der traditionellen japanischen und der modernen internationalen Architektur und stellt es darüber hinaus als Produkt einer bis heute aktiven internationalen Zusammenarbeit dar. Nicht zuletzt wird es auch als Zeichen der langjährigen engen Verbindung zwischen dem Museum für Angewandte Kunst Frankfurt und der japanischen Kultur verstanden.
Viele Menschen, Firmen und Institutionen haben bei der Realisierung des Gebäudes mitgearbeitet. Ihrem Engagement ist es zu verdanken, dass wir nun über ein wertvolles Kunstobjekt der Breathing Architecture verfügen.
Wir danken ihnen auf der nebenstehenden Tabula gratiarum. Kengo Kuma und seinen Mitarbeitern sei Dank für ihre herrliche Idee und ihre Freundschaft.
Dem Birkhäuser Verlag, Basel, Berlin, Boston danken wir für die engagierte, gewohnt zuverlässige und professionelle Zusammenarbeit.

Prof. Dr. Ulrich Schneider, Direktor des Museums für Angewandte Kunst Frankfurt

Prof. Dr. Volker Fischer, Kurator der Abteilung Design am Museum für Angewandte Kunst Frankfurt

Dr. Stephan Graf v. d. Schulenburg, Kurator für die Kunst des Mittleren und des Fernen Osten am Museum für Angewandte Kunst Frankfurt

Kengo Kuma
What is a Teahouse?
Gedanken zum Teehaus

Furuta Oribe: En'an teahouse, garden,
Kyōto, circa 1640/55
Furuta Oribe: En'an Teehaus, Garten,
Kyōto, um 1640/55

Haruki Murakami, one of Japan's most famous novelists, once said that when he is writing a full-length novel, he feels the desire to write a short story, and the reverse when he is writing a short story. From my point of view, a teahouse is like a short story. Murakami writes:

"As a writer, a short story for me represents an important venue where I can learn, and continue the pursuit of what I am looking for. This may be the same type of thing as a design for an artist" (A Young Reader's Guide to Short Fiction)[1].

When Murakami is writing a short story, and begins to feel that there is something left to say beyond the scope of this form, he heads off towards writing a full-length novel. For example, after writing *Hotaru* (Firefly), he then penned *Noruwei no mori* (Norwegian Wood)[2], to relay something for which there was no room in the short story.

To anticipate my conclusion, creating a short story — here, a teahouse — is an important matter for an architect; and this is the topic of this article. However, I do feel that the affair of the teahouse is rather more complicated and arduous. But in what way is it complicated? I should like first to consider the increasing complexity and globality of the social and economic circumstances in relation to architecture.

Last year, I was involved in the development of Tōkyō Midtown, a gigantic construction project. Being involved in such a huge development project was significant for two reasons: the first was its alarmingly tight schedule, and the other was having to build something that could be resold. I came to understand that with this type of project you

Haruki Murakami, einer der bekanntesten japanischen Romanciers unserer Zeit, hat einmal gesagt, dass er beim Schreiben eines langen Romans Lust bekomme, eine Kurzgeschichte zu schreiben, und umgekehrt beim Schreiben einer Kurzgeschichte Lust bekomme, einen langen Roman zu schreiben. Für mich ist das Teehaus wie eine Kurzgeschichte.

In diesem Zusammenhang bemerkt Murakami: „Für mich als Schriftsteller ist [die Kurzgeschichte] immer ein wichtiges Feld des Lernens und Forschens gewesen. Ich könnte auch sagen, dass sie für mich so etwas wie die Skizze für den Maler ist."[1]

Wenn Murakami beim Verfassen einer Kurzgeschichte das Gefühl hat, dass da noch ein Rest bleibt, der sich in diesem beschränkten Format nicht ausdrücken lässt, wendet er sich dem langen Roman zu. So entstand nach der Kurzgeschichte *Hotaru* („Leuchtkäfer") der Roman *Noruwei no mori* („Der norwegische Wald")[2], in dem das ausgeführt wird, was in jener Kurzgeschichte keinen Platz gefunden hatte.

Um hier gleich den Schluss vorwegzunehmen, auch für den Architekten ist die Kurzgeschichte, das heißt der Bau eines Teehauses, eine wichtige Angelegenheit, und das ist auch das Thema dieses Essays.

Allerdings habe ich das Gefühl, dass die Sache beim Teehaus noch etwas mühsamer und komplizierter ist. Doch was ist daran so kompliziert? Im Zusammenhang mit der Architektur möchte ich deshalb zuerst auf die zunehmende Komplexität und Globalität der wirtschaftlichen und gesellschaftlichen Verhältnisse eingehen.

Letztes Jahr war ich am Bau von Tōkyō Midtown, einem gigantischen Immobilienprojekt, beteiligt. Die Beteiligung an einem

[1] Murakami Haruki: Wakai dokusha no tame no tanpenshōsetsu-annai (A Young Reader's Guide to Short Fiction). In: Bungei shunjū, 1997.
[2] Murakami Haruki: Hotaru (Firefly), 1983, Engl. in The Elephant Vanishes, 1994.
Murakami Haruki: Noruwei no mori, 1987; Norwegian Wood, 1989.

[1] Murakami Haruki: Wakai dokusha no tame no tanpenshō-setsu-annai („Kurzgeschichten-Führer für junge Leser"). In: Bungei shunjū, 1997.
[2] Ders.: Hotaru („Leuchtkäfer"), dt. in: Wie ich eines schönen Morgens im April das 100%ige Mädchen sah, 1996.
Ders.: Noruwei no mori, 1987; dt. Der norwegische Wald.

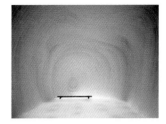

cannot proceed at a leisurely pace, and that the people involved had to comply with a tight schedule since the whole thing was so enormous. Such a huge project, the total cost of which was measured in hundreds of billions of yen, naturally also battles against incurring interest. A single day's delay can easily cost tens or hundreds of million yen. There is a continual race against time for both the design and construction work. I designed two buildings — the Suntory Museum of Art and the restaurant building called "Garden Terrace". Work on the foundations started before the design work was completed. And when I wanted to try out a new detail or type of material, time was always the problem. The only way to proceed with the design was to cut and paste existing detail features that had already proved reliable. This gave me first-hand experience of how socioeconomic constraints produce today's endemic, boring architecture, which combines things that you have already seen somewhere else. The only countermeasures against this inevitability are details and materials of proven reliability. If you don't have such trump cards up your sleeve, it is impossible to win this battle. To meet the extreme challenges of such a huge project, you have to have a few "secret weapons". Otherwise, even with great architectural talent and sensitivity, the storm just blows you away.

But this does not mean that you should prepare such "secret weapons" for a particular project; it is enough to have some in reserve. For example, I had a technique for using ceramics — a material that is difficult to process — in vertical louvers, making the slats of the louver very narrow. We used the same terracotta material as

SOM[3] for the facade of the skyscraper towers, but applied them to the aluminum louver slats as an ultrathin 8 mm coating. The Paulownia wood (*kiri*)[4] and Japanese paper materials (*washi*), which we had used for interior decoration throughout the Suntory Museum of Art, and which are soft and tricky to handle, are used in the teahouse as the result of a long process of trial and error. This is why we can withstand the extreme stress of any large-scale project: without these "secret weapons" at our disposal, we would undoubtedly have been overwhelmed by and swept away from the project's storm of global changes.

The teahouse is an element that has always been outside the pace of the contemporary economy, standing separate and alone. Compared to the unfathomable scale of the economy, it may appear negligible. This is why it is a place where you can relax... and take on the risk of experimenting. However, a place which is a little on the outside is somewhere where you can create a secret weapon that is valuable on the inside. This mind-set is almost the same as the mindset of a terrorist. In order to fight against globalism in architecture, the small teahouse is our hide-out, where we plan our strategy like a terrorist.

In fact, the situation in 16th- and 17th-century Japan, when the "teahouse style" made its appearance, is extremely similar to the circumstances with which we are confronted today. First, there was increasing trade with China and the Korean peninsula, a large volume of china and pottery made in China and Korea was being imported, and many artisans who made these products

Kengo Kuma: Oribe Teahouse (temporary exhibition pavilion), Ceramics Park Mino, Tajimi, Gifu, 2005, and exhibition "ArchiLab Japon" Galerie d'Art Contemporain, Orléans, France, 2006
Kengo Kuma: Oribe-Teehaus (temporärer Ausstellungspavillon), Keramik-Park Mino, Tajimi, Gifu, 2005, und Ausstellung „ArchiLab Japon" Galerie d'Art Contemporain, Orléans, Frankreich, 2006

Interior, details of synthetic ribs and strap links, A-A section (p. 11)
Innenansicht, Details Kunststoffrippen und Verbindungsbänder, A-A-Schnitt (S. 11)

---

[3] SOM: internationally active architectural office with headquarters in Chicago, USA.
[4] Soft, light wood (Paulownia serrata), famous in Japan for its use for wooden boxes, i.e. storage for tea ceremony equipment and art.

Furuta Oribe: En'an Teahouse, Kyōto, circa 1640/55

Furuta Oribe: En'an Teehaus, um 1640/55

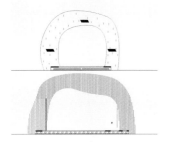

solchen Großprojekt ist in zweierlei Hinsicht bedeutsam: Erstens ist der Zeitrahmen dabei erschreckend knapp und rigoros. Zweitens muss man etwas bauen, was sich auch weiterverkaufen lässt. Weil das Ganze so riesige Dimensionen hat, kann man dabei nicht gründlich arbeiten. Im Gegenteil, ich habe begriffen, dass die schiere Größe des Projekts den Beteiligten einen unglaublich harten Zeitplan abverlangt. Ein solches Megaprojekt, bei dem die Gesamtkosten in die Hunderte von Millionen Euro gehen, ist natürlich auch ein Kampf mit den Zinsen. Wenn die Fertigstellung sich auch nur um einen einzigen Tag verzögert, kostet das gleich mehrere Millionen Euro. Planung und Bauarbeiten werden zum Kampf gegen die Zeit. Ich selbst habe bei diesem Projekt das neue Suntory Museum und das „Gartenterrasse" benannte Restaurantgebäude entworfen. Doch während ich noch an den Plänen arbeitete, fingen schon die Arbeiten am Fundament an, ohne dass man auf mich Rücksicht genommen hätte. Auch wenn man irgendwelche neuen Detailelemente oder Baumaterialien ausprobieren will, scheitert das an Zeitmangel. Es bleibt keine andere Wahl, als bewährte, vorhandene Standarddetails im Copy-Paste-Verfahren einzusetzen. So habe ich am eigenen Leib erfahren müssen, wie sozioökonomische Zwänge zu der vorherrschenden langweiligen Architektur führen, bei der einfach irgendwelche Dinge kombiniert werden, die man schon irgendwo gesehen zu haben scheint. Um dieser Situation gegenzusteuern, muss man ein paar besondere Detailelemente und Materialien, deren Zuverlässigkeit geprüft ist, zur Hand haben. Wenn man keine solchen Trumpfkarten im Ärmel verborgen hat, kann man in diesem Kampf nicht bestehen. Will man den extremen Anforderungen eines Mammutprojekts standhalten, so muss man ein paar „Geheimwaffen" besitzen. Sonst wird man selbst mit noch so viel architektonischer Begabung und Sensibilität von diesem Sturm einfach weggefegt werden.

Das bedeutet aber nicht, dass man solche „Geheimwaffen" speziell für ein bestimmtes Projekt vorbereiten müsste. Es genügt, sie für den Ernstfall in Reserve zu haben. So verfügte ich zum Beispiel über das Wissen, ansonsten schwierig zu bearbeitende Keramik in einer Art vertikalem Lamellenverbund mit schmaler Ansichtskante der Lamellen zu detaillieren. Wir benutzten dasselbe Terrakotta-Material wie SOM[3] in den Hochhausfassaden, jedoch in einer extrem dünnen Beschichtung von 8 mm Stärke auf die Aluminiumlamellen aufgebracht. Schwierig zu handhabendes, weiches Material aus *kiri*-Holz[4] oder *washi* (traditionelles Japanpapier), das wir beim Suntory Museum für die gesamte Innendekoration benutzt haben, ist das Ergebnis praktischer Langzeitanwendung und -überprüfung im Teehaus. Deshalb konnten wir damit unter den extremen Belastungen jenes Großprojekts bestehen. Ohne diese „Geheimwaffen" hätte der übermächtige Sturm globaler Veränderungen auch uns mit sich fortgerissen.

Als isoliertes, einsames Bauwerk steht das Teehaus auch außerhalb der gegenwärtigen Veränderungen. Wenn man es mit den unfasslichen Dimensionen der globalen Wirtschaft vergleicht, ist sein Wert in Zahlen vielleicht nur winzig. Aber gerade deshalb kann man hier großzügig sein und mit einem höheren Risiko experimentieren. Gerade an einem solchen weltfernen Ort kann man im Verborgenen etwas herstellen,

---

[3] SOM: weltweit tätiges Architektur- und Ingenieurbüro mit Hauptsitz in Chicago.
[4] Helles, weiches und leichtes Holz des Blauglockenbaums (Paulownia serrata); in Japan beliebtes Material für Holzkästen, z.B. zur Aufbewahrung von Teegerät und Kunstgegenständen.

immigrated to Japan. In addition, Francisco de Xavier (1506-1552)[5] and various other Jesuit missionaries came to Japan, representing an onslaught of Western religion, culture and technology at a time when Japan was an isolated island nation.

These changes produced a kind of cultural confusion. During and after World War II, culture and technology from overseas likewise came to Japan and created considerable confusion. The process of globalization brought about by the IT revolution since the 1990s has further accelerated this phenomenon.

The Japanese people in the 16th century created new culture consisting of such elements as the "teahouse," sukiya[6] and wabi-sabi[7] aesthetic of transience. What these people did can be considered a reorganization of all products, taking the human body as a reference. At the time, a virtually infinite number of new products had flowed into Japan. Their response was an attempt to reorganize all products using the body as a universal reference. They thought that referring to anything else would only add to the confusion. Therefore, they mercilessly discarded the traditional standards and cultural hierarchy used in Japan up to then. The teahouse is thus an exceedingly avant-garde type of architecture at the time. The "tea way of life" had an inherently subversive quality, with the potential to negate all tradition. This is why Hideyoshi, the supreme leader at this time, ordered Sen no Rikyū, the cultural leader of the "tea cultural movement," to commit ritual suicide by disembowelment.

Just what did the people of the time do to make the body the one and only standard? They started by creating a space where a person could focus his or her mind and truly feel his or her body. This space was the teahouse. Even when you tell someone to focus their mind on their body, unless that person has a lot of experience in meditation or is an expert at yoga, body and mind will remain separate from one another. However, if you provide a special type of space and place, the person in that space may find it possible to integrate body and mind. That special space was the "teahouse". First, they discovered that making the space small was an effective means of enabling people to focus their mind on their body.

They found out that when a person is placed in a space where the walls are right in front of your eyes, where the ceiling is so low that you hit your head if you stand up, distractions tend to leave the mind, and you are able to focus your mind on your body. The small entrance, called the nijiriguchi, or crawling-in entrance, further enhances this effect. This entrance measured only 60 x 60 cm, and forced the person to bend right over when entering the teahouse, and was thus the ultimate device to make an individual focus on the size of his or her body and its lack of free movement.

On some level, this orientation towards "smallness" went against the trends of the 16th century, one of which consisted of people becoming substantially more affluent as agricultural technology improved and commerce became more active, and this was reflected in larger living spaces. The same trend can be seen in contemporary Japan. As people become more affluent, the amount of residential space naturally increases. The living space in Japan has continued to increase since World War II.

Kengo Kuma: Teahouse, Shizuoka Convention Centre, 2007; elevation, interior details, structural elevation of vinyl balloon filled with helium and Super Organza membrane (p. 13)
Kengo Kuma: Teehaus, Shizuoka Convention Centre, 2007; Ansicht, Innenraumdetails, Strukturansicht Vinylballon mit Heliumfüllung und Überwurf aus Superorganza (S. 13)

---

[5] Francisco de Xavier, commonly known in English as St Francis Xavier, was a Spanish pioneering Roman Catholic Christian missionary in Asia and cofounder of the Society of Jesus (Jesuit Order) and the first Catholic missionary in Japan from 1549 to 1552.

[6] The sukiya style, which dates from 17th-century Japan, is generally regarded as one of the culminations of Japanese architecture and has influenced well-known architects of the 20th century.

[7] wabi-sabi: refer to the article by Schulenburg in this publication.

Sen no Rikyū: Tai'an teahouse, Myōki'an
temple, Kyōto, 1582 – the covered
walkway to the teahouse, wall detail
Sen no Rikyū: Tai'an Teahaus, Myōki'an
Tempel, Kyōto, 1582 – der überdachte
Weg zum Teehaus, Wanddetail

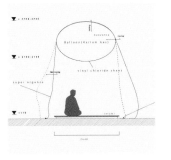

das innerhalb der heutigen Welt ihren Wert hat. Um die Globalisierung in der Architektur zu bekämpfen, verbarrikadieren wir uns in unserer geheimen Operationsbasis, dem Teehaus. Diese Geisteshaltung ist mit der von Terroristen vergleichbar.

In Wirklichkeit waren die Zustände im Japan des 16. und 17. Jahrhunderts, als der „Teehausstil" aufkam, den heutigen Verhältnissen sehr ähnlich. Damals nahm der Warenaustausch mit China und der koreanischen Halbinsel stark zu, und vor allem Keramik aus China und Korea wurde in großen Mengen nach Japan eingeführt. Auch koreanische und chinesische Töpfer sind in beträchtlicher Zahl nach Japan übergesiedelt. Außerdem kamen, angefangen mit Francisco de Xavier (1506—1552)[5], jesuitische Missionare nach Japan, und plötzlich drangen europäische Religion, Kultur und Technik in jenes isolierte Inselreich ein.

Diese Veränderungen führten zu einer Art kultureller Verwirrung. Auch nach dem Zweiten Weltkrieg breiteten sich westliche Kultur und Technologie in Japan aus und verursachten eine ziemliche Konfusion. Die Globalisierung, die von den 1990er Jahren an durch die IT-Revolution ausgelöst wurde, hat diese Veränderungen noch beschleunigt. Die Japaner des 16. Jahrhunderts haben aus dieser Verwirrung heraus neue Kultur- und Kunstformen wie Teehaus, *sukiya*[6] und *wabi-sabi*[7] entwickelt. Um ihre damalige Leistung in einem Wort zusammenzufassen, so bestand sie darin, alle Produkte auf Grundlage des menschlichen Körpers neu zu vermessen. Zu jener Zeit waren zahllose neue Dinge nach Japan eingeströmt, und so wurde versucht, das Neue mit dem universalen Grundmaß des menschlichen Körpers in Beziehung zu setzen und noch einmal neu

zu ordnen. Die Menschen jener Zeit erkannten, dass es nur zu noch größerem Chaos führen würde, wenn man sich auf ein anderes Grundmaß verließe. Deshalb verwarfen sie schonungslos die bisherigen traditionellen Maßstäbe und kulturellen Hierarchien Japans. Im damaligen Japan verkörperte das Teehaus eine unglaublich avantgardistische Architektur. Im Teeweg wohnte ein subversiver Geist inne, der sich nicht scheute, die Tradition insgesamt zu negieren. Deshalb musste Sen no Rikyū (1521-1591), der geistige Führer der Teekultur-Bewegung, auf Befehl Toyotomi Hideyoshis (1536-1598), des mächtigsten Führers jener Zeit, Selbstmord begehen.

Wie sind nun die Menschen jener Zeit vorgegangen, um den menschlichen Körper zum alleinigen Maßstab zu machen? Als Erstes schufen sie einen Raum, in dem sich das Bewusstsein im Körper sammeln ließ und sich des Körpers bewusst wurde. Dieser Raum war das Teehaus. Auch wenn man dem Geist befiehlt, sich im Körper zu sammeln, werden Körper und Bewusstsein gewöhnlich getrennt bleiben, außer man ist ein großer Joga-Meister oder hat genügend meditative Erfahrungen gesammelt. Doch wenn man einen besonderen Raum bereitstellt, können Körper und Geist eins werden. Dieser besondere Raum ist das Teehaus. Zuerst haben die Teemeister entdeckt, dass die Verkleinerung des Raums ein wirkungsvolles Mittel ist, um das Bewusstsein auf den Körper zu lenken. Im Teehaus setzt man sich in einen Raum, in dem man die Wand unmittelbar vor Augen hat und die Decke so niedrig ist, dass man beim Aufstehen fast mit dem Kopf dagegenstößt. Die Teemeister hatten auch bemerkt, dass

[5] Francisco de Xavier: im deutschsprachigen Raum bekannt als der Heilige Franz Xaver, Pionier der christlichen Mission in Asien und Mitbegründer der Gesellschaft Jesu; von 1549 bis 1552 als erster katholischer Missionar in Japan.
[6] Der so genannte *sukiya*-Stil gilt als Gipfelpunkt der traditionellen japanischen Wohnarchitektur und hat viele große Architekten des 20. Jahrhunderts beeinflusst.
[7] *wabi-sabi*: vgl. Beitrag Schulenburg in dieser Publikation.

The "teahouse" was born from a countertrend, a serious attempt to reverse the increase in space from the Middle Ages to the 16th century. Sen no Rikyū was particularly zealous in his pursuit of decreasing the amount of space. His masterpiece, the Taian Teahouse[8], which has been declared a national treasure, measures only two *daime tatami*[9] mats. Since a *daime* is equal to $3/4$ of a *tatami* mat, this produces a space that measures approximately 1.8 x 2.7 m. The tea master and the guest would enter this tiny space together, sit down, fold their legs neatly, boil the water, place the powdered tealeaves in the hot water, mix it vigorously and then slowly pour the thick, bitter liquid into the depth of their bodies.

This type of ceremony, performed in this tiny space, erased the thoughts of everyday life, enabling the body and mind to become one.

This special space was not just simply small. While enclosing the body, it also was an attempt to bring nature into the space. Although at first it seemed impossible to incorporate the great outdoors in this space, they were able to introduce a small slice of nature. They discovered that the person entering this tiny piece of nature reacts much more strongly due to the heightened level of sensitivity that this tiny space engenders. Nature and the body resonate with one another, noises and agitation are eliminated from the body, and the body is reset and refreshed.

Various mechanisms were devised to incorporate nature into the teahouse. These included a criticism of the *shoin-zukuri*[10] style of architecture, which was the dominant representational architectural style of that

time. Today, *shoin-zukuri* would be called modern architecture. The structure is an orderly grid system, and the space was open and flexible. Artificial materials that were straight and flat were preferred. The result is the type of universal space that was proposed by Mies van der Rohe. In contrast to this, the proponents of the teahouse wanted space that was irregular and organic.

For example, the provision of a filtered window at the bottom of the wall called a *shitaji-mado* indicated the presence of nature. The power of the imagination would be lost if all of the elements outside the teahouse were shown, and the body would become negligent. With only a hint of the presence of nature, the body becomes more sensitive and is stimulated. This creates a number of subtle, refined relationships between the outdoors and the indoors.

As far as materials were concerned, natural materials were preferred over man-made ones. However, rather than excessively vivid nature, the tea masters used materials and details throughout the teahouse that just gave off a hint of nature. The earth walls used in Sen no Rikyū's Taian Teahouse are representative of this attempt to provide a hint of nature. A large volume of plant fibers called *susa* were mixed in and used in the earth walls, which were similar to the coarse, rough walls in poor farmhouses. The green *susa* fibers disappeared when the walls were painted black, leaving only aspects that would further stimulate the power of imagination.

In addition, rather than giving the earth walls sharp right angles, they were finished with soft curved surfaces. The teahouse

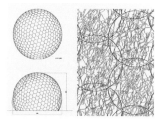

Kengo Kuma: K x K (Kuma x Krug) (temporary exhibition pavilion), Hara Museum, Shinagawa-ku, Tōkyō, 2004/05 — elevations with construction details of the EVA membrane, a membrane with temperature-dependent shrinkage coefficients, total elevation
Kengo Kuma: K x K (Kuma x Krug) (temporärer Ausstellungspavillon), Hara Museum, Shinagawa-ku, Tōkyō, 2004/05 — Ansichten mit Konstruktionsdetails des Membranmaterials EVA, eine Membran mit temperaturabhängigen Schrumpfungskoeffizienten, Gesamtansicht

---

[8] This teahouse from 1582 is now in the Myōki'an Zen temple in Kyōto. The world of Rikyū is still present on just two *tatami* mats.
[9] Two *tatami-daime*: A special size of *tatami* called *daime* is often used for tearooms. In addition to the floor area of two *tatami*, there is a *tokonoma* (small raised alcove) and the *daime* extension of about $3/4$ of the *tatami*, used for the host and the tea equipment. The average size of a *tatami* mat is approximately 90 x 180 cm (approx. 1.6 m²).
[10] *shoin-zukuri*: style of Japanese representative architecture in the 14th to 16th century for aristocratic residences.

Kobori Enshū: Hassōnoseki Teahouse,
Konchi-in, Nanzen-ji, Kyōto, circa 1628 —
interiors
Kobori Enshū: Hassōnoseki-Teehaus,
Konchi-in, Nanzen-ji, Kyōto, um 1628 —
Innenansichten

an einem solchen Ort müßige Gedanken verschwinden und der Geist sich im Körper sammelt. Dazu trug auch der als *nijiriguchi* bezeichnete kleine Eingang bei. Diese Öffnung von etwa 60 x 60 cm Größe, durch die man nicht ins Innere gelangte, ohne auf die Knie zu gehen und hindurchzukriechen, war ein geschicktes Mittel, um die Dimension und die Eingeschränktheit des Körpers bewusst zu machen.

Diese Hinwendung zum „Kleinen" war in gewissem Sinne eine Gegenbewegung gegen die Strömungen jenes Zeitalters. Damals machte die Landwirtschaftstechnik Fortschritte, der Handel blühte auf und die Menschen wurden wohlhabender. Dementsprechend wurde auch der Wohnraum vergrößert und reicher ausgestattet. In unserer Zeit sehen wir eine ähnliche Entwicklung. Mit dem wachsenden Wohlstand hat sich der Wohnraum in Japan nach dem Zweiten Weltkrieg ständig vergrößert.

Die Kultivierung einer Geisteshaltung, die sich gegen den Strom der Zeit richtete, hatte zur Geburt des Teehauses geführt. Es war eine große Herausforderung, die Strömung umzukehren, die sich seit dem Mittelalter in Japan durchgesetzt hatte. Dabei setzte sich Sen no Rikyū besonders eifrig für die Verkleinerung des Raumes ein. Die Grundfläche des von ihm entworfenen Teehauses Tai'an[8], seines heute zum nationalen Kulturgut erklärten größten Meisterwerks, betrug lediglich zwei *tatami-daime*[9]. Da die Größe einer *tatami-daime* lediglich drei Viertel einer normalen *tatami* beträgt, ist die Fläche dieses Teehauses kleiner als drei *tatami*. Diesen winzigen Raum betreten Gastgeber und Gäste, Schulter an Schulter gedrängt, und nehmen Platz, indem sie sich säuberlich auf die gefalteten Beine setzen. Teewasser wird zum

Kochen gebracht, Pulver von Teeblättern in die Teeschale gegeben und mit überraschend energischer Bewegung verrührt. Gemächlich wird die kräftige, bittere Flüssigkeit getrunken und verteilt sich bis in die hintersten Winkel des Körpers. Bei diesem in sich geschlossenen Ritual, das auf winzigstem Raum abläuft, verschwinden die weltlichen Gedanken und Körper und Geist verschmelzen zu einer Einheit.

Dieser besondere Raum ist nicht einfach nur klein. Die Teemeister haben versucht, sogar die Natur in diesen von Gästen und Gastgeber ganz ausgefüllten, engen Raum hereinzuholen. Obwohl es zunächst unmöglich schien, die große Natur einzubeziehen, gelang es ihnen, ein kleines Stückchen Natur hereinzulassen. Man entdeckte nämlich, dass auf extrem engem Raum die Sinne geschärft werden und stärker auf äußere Reize reagieren. Natur und Körper schwingen im Einklang, Lärm und Unruhe im Körper kommen zur Ruhe, Körper und Geist finden zurück in ihren ursprünglichen Zustand.

Um die Natur ins Teehaus einzubeziehen, haben sich die Teeleute verschiedene Mittel ausgedacht, in denen sich auch eine Form von Kritik an dem damals vorherrschenden, repräsentativen Architekturstil, dem *shoin-zukuri*[10], der „modernen Architektur" jener Zeit, manifestierte. Die *shoin*-Architektur folgte einem regelmäßigen Rastersystem und zeichnete sich durch vollkommene Flexibilität und räumliche Offenheit aus. Zum Bauen bevorzugte man nach Möglichkeit geradliniges, flaches und bearbeitetes Material. Es entstand ein Raum, den Mies van der Rohe als „universal space" pries. Im Gegensatz dazu versuchte man mit dem Teehaus einen unregelmäßigen, organischen Raum zu gestalten.

---

[8] Dieses Teehaus aus dem Jahre 1582 steht heute im Zen-Tempel Myōki'an in Kyōto. Die ganze Welt Rikyūs ist dort auf nur zwei *tatami* lebendig.

[9] „Zwei *tatami-daime*" ist eine spezielle Grundrissform für sehr kleine Teehäuser, bei der zur Zwei-*tatami*-Fläche des eigentlichen Teeraums noch eine *tokonoma* und eine als *daime* bezeichnete Erweiterung um etwa drei Viertel *tatami* kommen, die für den Gastgeber und das Teegerät bestimmt ist. Die Durchschnittsmaße einer *tatami* betragen etwa 90 x 180 cm (etwa 1,6 m^2).

[10] *shoin-zukuri* — Shoin-Architektur: der vom 14. bis zum 16. Jahrhundert entwickelte repräsentative Baustil für (aristokratische) Residenzen in Japan.

thus negated the Cartesian grid, an expression that was the mirror opposite of the artificial *shoin* style of architecture, which was entirely made up of right angles; and was directly related to the body from the moment the body entered the space.

In our teahouse, we attempted to bring back the spirit of this special space called *chashitsu* in a contemporary manner. But just copying the style of the teahouse would be meaningless. The teahouse style of the 16th century was a criticism of the globalization that Japan experienced at that time, but we did not think our teahouse could serve as a weapon to fight against globalization in the 21st century. For that, we would need a weapon with both strength and sharpness.
And again we return to the human body as the one thing with the inner strength to stand up to this new wave of globalization. We have yet to find something with the definite presence of the body to serve as an effective weapon, and will be unlikely to find anything that exceeds it in the future. We looked at extremely small elements in order to pursue nature, in the same way as Sen no Rikyū, as the means to focus the mind on the body, and in turn foster a true realization of the body's potential. The result was this teahouse structure, which appears more like the body itself than an architectural construction. It has the delicacy of a body, but at the same time it is strong, and it even breathes. This Teahouse is brought to life by a new white material called Tenara[11]. In contrast, Sen no Rikyū's Tai'an Teahouse was dark and black. However, if Sen no Rikyū were alive today, and were to create a teahouse that matched contemporary trends, I think he would have made one that looked something like this. The spirit of the teahouse continues to live on. However, the way in which it does so will continue to manifest itself in new forms.

Fujimori Terunobu: "Takasugi'an"
(Too High Retreat), Chino, Nagano, 2004
— elevation and interior
Fujimori Terunobu: „Takasugi'an",
(Zu-Hoch-Klause), Chino, Nagano, 2004
— Ansicht und Innenansicht

[11] Tenara: refer to the article by Saikawa in this publication.

Tea preparation brush (*chasen*) used to
stir the pulverized green tea, from the
14th century onward
Tee-Schaumbesen (*chasen*) zum Rühren
des grünen Pulvertees, seit dem
14. Jahrhundert

Stirred pulverized tea (*matcha*)
Der gerührte Pulvertee (*matcha*)

Indem die Teeleute zum Beispiel an der Wand
eine kleine Öffnung mit Bambusgitter, das
so genannte *shitaji-mado*, anbrachten,
wurde der Teeraum für einen Hauch von
Natur geöffnet. Stünde das Teehaus jedoch
völlig offen für die äußere Natur, würde die
Fantasie eingeschränkt und der Körper
abgestumpft. Indem man sich auf die Andeu-
tung von Natur beschränkt, wird der Körper
dagegen sensibilisiert und aktiviert.
Zwischen dem Außenraum und dem Innenraum des Teehauses wurden auf solche Weise
zahlreiche subtile und raffinierte Verbindungen
geschaffen.

Für den Bau eines Teehauses bevorzugte
man natürliche Materialien statt der vor-
gefertigten, künstlichen Baustoffe wie beim
shoin-zukuri. Doch dabei suchten die Teemeister nicht die „rohe" Natur, sondern
wählten Materialien und Dekorelemente, die
im Teeraum eine gewisse natürliche Atmosphäre schufen. Die Lehmwand Sen no Rikyūs
in seinem Teehaus Taian ist repräsentativ
für dieses Streben. So mischte er große
Mengen von Pflanzenfasern (jap. *susa*)
unter den Lehm, und es entstand eine Wand,
die der rauen, schlecht gearbeiteten Lehmwand eines ärmlichen Bauernhauses glich.
Durch die Schwärzung der Wand brachte er
das rohe Grün der Pflanzenfasern zum
Verschwinden, und so konnte die Fantasie
sich umso besser entfalten.
Außerdem hat er die Übergänge zwischen
den Lehmwänden nicht mit scharfen rechten
Winkeln ausgeführt, sondern weiche,
gebogene Formen benutzt. Diese Form der
Gestaltung, die im Gegensatz zur generell
rechtwinkligen, kunstvollen *shoin*-Architektur
steht, überträgt sich direkt auf den Körper,
sobald er den Teeraum betritt.

Mit unserem Teehaus haben wir versucht,
das besondere Raumgefühl des klassischen
chashitsu in unserer modernen Zeit neu zu
beleben. Lediglich den traditionellen Stil des
Teehauses kopieren zu wollen, wäre sinnlos.
Der Teehausstil hatte die Funktion, Kritik an
der Globalisierung Japans im 16. Jahrhundert
zum Ausdruck zu bringen. Aber wir hätten
uns zunächst nicht vorstellen können, dass
sich unser Teehaus zur Waffe gegen die
Globalisierung des 21. Jahrhunderts eignen
würde. Was wir brauchen, um dagegen
anzugehen, ist eine Waffe, die Stärke und
Schärfe in sich vereint.

Die Basis, von der aus wir diesen Kampf
führen, ist wiederum der menschliche
Körper. Wir haben immer noch keine andere
Waffe entdeckt, die über die Effektivität
unseres realen Daseins hinausgeht, und das
wird auch in Zukunft so bleiben. Wie Sen no
Rikyū haben wir das extrem Kleine gesucht
und die Natur erforscht, um das Bewusstsein im Körper zu sammeln und uns des
Potenzials unseres Körpers wirklich bewusst
zu werden. Als Ergebnis entstand dieses
Teehaus, das eher wie ein lebendiger Orga-
nismus als eine architektonische Konstruktion
aussieht. Es ist zugleich delikat und kraft-
voll wie ein lebender Körper, und es atmet.
Während unser Teehaus aus Tenara[11], einem
modernen weißen Gewebe, gefertigt ist, war
Sen no Rikyūs Teehütte Tai'an düster und
schwarz. Würde er heute noch leben und mit
den Strömungen unserer Zeit in Berührung
kommen, so hätte wohl auch er ein ähnliches
Bauwerk errichtet. Der Geist des Teehauses
lebt weiter, aber er wird sich immer wieder
in neuen Formen manifestieren.

[11] Tenara: vgl. Beitrag Saikawa in dieser Publikation.

Ulrich Schneider

Breathing Architecture — Building for Nomads?

Breathing Architecture — Baukunst für Nomaden?

Kengo Kuma: teahouse design. 2007
Kengo Kuma: Entwurf für das Teehaus.
2007

1

On May 15, 2005, the Japanese architect
Kengo Kuma visited the Museum of
Applied Arts in Frankfurt. Miki Shimokawa,
a freelance curator active in Germany and
Japan, had arranged his visit. With great
interest Kuma admired the buildings by
Richard Meier, the classicistic villa, and also
the glorious park, which is an important
element in Meier's architectural concept.
Kuma was especially drawn to a gentle, treed
hill near the restaurant patio.

At the end of the visit, which naturally included
a tour of the collections and in particular
the Japanese section, Kengo Kuma announced
that the small knoll in the park would make
an ideal site for a Japanese teahouse.
He bade everyone farewell and traveled on
towards Wiesbaden for a visit to the spa.
A short while later we received computer
generated sketches of a building from
Tōkyō: it was clearly tailored from a semi-
transparent textile material and formed
two connected, pneumatic igloo shapes.

Over the course of the following two years,
an intense collaboration ensued between
Kengo Kuma & Associates (Tōkyō) as designers, formTL ingenieure für tragwerk und
leichtbau gmbH (Radolfzell) as consultants
and engineers, Takenaka Europe GmbH
(Düsseldorf) as general contractors for the
foundation, Canobbio S.p.A. (Castelnuovo
Scrivia) as creators of the membrane and
Gustav Nolting GmbH (Detmold) as manufacturers of the compressed air system on
the one hand and the building authorities
of the city of Frankfurt am Main as well as
the curators of the Museum of Applied Arts
Frankfurt on the other.

1

Am 15. Mai 2005 besuchte der japanische
Architekt Kengo Kuma das Museum für
Angewandte Kunst Frankfurt. Vermittelt
wurde seine Visite von der in Deutschland
und Japan tätigen freien Kuratorin Miki
Shimokawa. Mit großem Interesse bewunderte
Kuma die Bauten Richard Meiers, die
klassizistische Villa, aber auch den herrlichen
Park, der wichtiger Bestandteil des Architektur-
konzeptes von Richard Meier ist. Besonders
angezogen fühlte sich Kuma von einem
sachten, baumbestandenen Hügel nahe der
Restaurantterrasse.

Am Ende des Besuches, der natürlich auch
durch die Sammlungen und speziell durch
deren japanische Abteilung führte, teilte
Kengo Kuma mit, dass die kleine Anhöhe
im Park der ideale Standort für ein japanisches
Teehaus wäre. Dann verabschiedete er sich,
um in Wiesbaden die Thermen zu besuchen.
Schon kurze Zeit später erreichten uns aus
Tōkyō computergenerierte Skizzen eines
Gebäudes, das offensichtlich aus halb trans-
parentem Textil geschneidert war und sich,
luftgestützt, in zwei verbundene Igluformen
erhob.
In den folgenden zwei Jahren entwickelte
sich eine intensive Zusammenarbeit zwischen
Kengo Kuma & Associates (Tōkio) als
Entwerfer, formTL ingenieure für tragwerk
und leichtbau gmbH (Radolfzell) als
Berater und Planer, Takenaka Europe GmbH
(Düsseldorf) als Generalunternehmer
Fundament, Canobbio S.p.A. (Castelnuovo
Scrivia) als Konfektionär der Membranhülle
und Gustav Nolting GmbH (Detmold) als
Hersteller für das Druckluftgebläse auf der
einen Seite und dem Hochbauamt der Stadt
Frankfurt am Main sowie den Kuratoren des

The outcome of this cooperation is a unique building: a concreted and white lacquered foundation slab, roughly in the shape of a figure of eight and with a length of 8.3 m and a width of 4.4 m is the basis. At the center a rectangular depression accommodates nine *tatami* mats as well as a square *irori* fire pit for an electric hot plate. This foundation slab is surrounded by a sheet metal box covered in strong acryl panels and through the center of which runs an LED ribbon. Weather stripping is screwed onto the inner and outer edges of the metal box. Large zippers pulled into the channels of these strips serve to attach the textile structure of the inflatable building to the foundation slab.

formTL was charged with the difficult task of computing the precise form of this object composed of a hermetically closed inner and outer membrane and self-supporting without airlock modules. Kengo Kuma & Associates had stipulated that a somewhat taller igloo shape with a small *nijiriguchi* opening as a guest room and a lower igloo with a large door as preparation room were to be linked by a saddle-like connection: as a whole, the form is best compared to that of a peanut shell cut in half lengthwise.

In computing this structure the fundamental question arose whether the inner and outer membrane should be constructed as a series of tori in the manner of a Michelin man or as a point connection with the surface of a golf ball. Aesthetic considerations favored the latter option. Following experimentation over some time, a decision was made to choose the white, entirely odor-neutral GORE™ TENARA® Architectural Fabric 3T40, which is moreover semitransparent in the manner of *shōji* paper windows (and doors), as a membrane material. For the inner and outer membrane, precise sections were thermally linked. A complex system of anchors makes it possible to connect the two skins across a distance with textile straps that are then joined at the base. The calculation of the distance between the two membranes was extremely difficult because it cannot remain identical all around but must increase in concert with the height of the building.

Thus the width of the metal box surround of 0.4 m is sufficient as a basic interstitial gap, while the distance between the maximum inner (2.4 m) and the outer ridge height (3.1 m) must be a respectable 1 m in order to guarantee storm-proof load-bearing for a continuous air pressure of 1,500 Pascal.

Uncharted territory also had to be explored with regard to the pneumatic air generator because a dehumidification system and absolute silence, which is essential for a tea ceremony, were prerequisites for the construction. The task was therefore to develop a highly baffled mobile apparatus, which is set up some 20 m from the teahouse. It blows warm and dehumidified air through a subterranean duct- and above-ground hose system to the inflation nozzles at the teahouse.

After two-and-a-half years of design, permit applications and construction, the structure was installed for the first time on July 2, 2007. The textile membrane, with an approximate weight of 180 kg, was transported to the cleaned foundation, pulled into position and

FormTL: structural design. 2006
FormTL: Konstruktionsentwurf. 2006

Museums für Angewandte Kunst Frankfurt auf der anderen Seite.

Ergebnis dieser Kooperation ist ein einzigartiges Gebäude: Die Basis stellt eine betonierte und weiß lackierte Grundplatte dar, deren Form einer Acht ähnelt, mit einer Länge von 8,3 und einer Breite von 4,4 Meter. In deren Zentrum nimmt eine rechteckige Eintiefung neun *tatami*-Matten sowie die quadratische *irori*-Feuerkuhle für eine Elektrokochplatte auf. Diese Grundplatte wird von einem Blechkasten gesäumt, der mit starken Acrylplatten abgedeckt ist und in dessen Mitte ein LED-Band verläuft. Auf den Innen- und den Außenrand dieses Blechkastens sind Kederprofile aufgeschraubt. In deren Nuten werden die großen Reißverschlüsse eingezogen, mit deren Hilfe die textile Struktur des aufblasbaren Gebäudes fest mit der Grundplatte verbunden wird.

formTL fiel die schwierige Aufgabe zu, die genaue Form dieses ohne Luftschleuse selbsttragenden Objektes aus geschlossener Innen- und Außenhülle zu berechnen. Kengo Kuma & Associates hatten festgelegt, dass eine höhere Igluform mit kleinem *nijiriguchi*-Durchschlupf als Gastraum und eine niedrigere mit großer Tür als Vorbereitungsraum durch eine sattelartige Verbindung vereint sein sollten: eine Gesamtform, die am besten mit der halbierten Schale einer Erdnuss verglichen werden kann.

Bei der Berechnung dieser Struktur stellte sich die grundsätzliche Frage, ob Innen- und Außenhaut als Wulstfolge in der Art des Michelin-Männchens oder als Punktverbindung mit der Oberfläche eines Golfballs konstruiert werden sollten. Ästhetische Bewertungen sprachen für die zweite Möglichkeit.

Als Material wurde nach längeren Versuchen das weiße, in der Art von *shōji*-Papierfenstern (und -türen) halb transparente, vollkommen geruchsneutrale GORE™ TENARA® Architectural Fabric 3T40 bestimmt. Für Innen- und Außenhaut wurden exakte Bahnschnitte thermisch verbunden. Ein komplexes System von Ankerpunkten ermöglicht die distanzierte Verbindung von beiden Häuten mit Textilbändern, die schließlich am Fußpunkt vereinigt wurden. Große Schwierigkeit bot die Berechnung der Distanz der beiden Häute, die nicht gleich sein darf, sondern bei steigender Höhe des Gebäudes wachsen muss.

So genügt als Basisdistanz die Breite des Blechkastensaums von 0,4 Meter, während die Distanz von maximaler innerer (2,4 m) und äußerer Firsthöhe (3,4 m) immerhin 1 Meter betragen muss, um eine sturmfeste Tragfähigkeit bei kontinuierlichem Luftdruck von 1500 Pascal zu garantieren.

Neuland musste auch bei dem Stützlufterzeuger betreten werden, denn zur Voraussetzung für die Konstruktion wurden eine Entfeuchtungsanlage und absolute Geräuschlosigkeit, die bei einer Teezeremonie unabdingbar ist. So galt es, einen hochgradig gedämpften mobilen Apparat zu entwickeln, der in etwa 20 Meter Entfernung vom Teehaus installiert wird. Er bläst Luft gewärmt und entfeuchtet über ein unterirdisches Röhren- und ein oberirdisches Schlauchsystem zum Einblasstutzen am Teehaus.

Nach zweieinhalbjährigen Planungs-, Genehmigungs- und Bauarbeiten konnte am 2. Juli 2007 die erste Installierung des Gebäudes stattfinden. Die circa 180 Kilogramm schwere Textilmembran wurde auf das gereinigte Fundament transportiert, eingezogen

inflated. Twenty minutes later the structure stood fully inflated and had lost none of the visionary character of the first computer simulation. It seemed to breathe like a living being. This was also the reason why the philosophical term weak architecture changed into breathing architecture, almost on its own. On its very first day, the teahouse withstood a heavy thunder storm, which provided an opportunity to also test the storage preparations. The membrane must never be deflated and folded when wet. Hence, the membrane and the air pump were transported from the park into the museum entrance hall, reinflated and cleaned where necessary. After approximately one hour of drying time, the air was once again deflated until a vacuum condition was reached; the membrane was then folded according to a predetermined pattern and moved to its storage location.

After this preparatory stage and the installation of the tea path with twenty-two granite steps and two basins, the teahouse was ready to be officially inaugurated on August 18, 2007. Increasingly familiar with the routine, the four-member installation team is now able to erect the teahouse on top of the carefully scrubbed floor slab in a matter of two hours, roll out the *tatami* mats across a rubber insulation layer, install the electric fire pit, set up the asymmetrical screen from Kyōto and attach a 300-year-old bamboo vase, which serves as a *tokonoma* niche, to the largest curvature in the guest area. A second indentation in the ground, accommodating all electric installations for the tea master, is located behind the screen which separates the guest room from the preparation area. Everything is ready for the tea ceremony to begin.

2

Kengo Kuma's teahouse is notable for its transcendental power, resulting on the one hand from an interplay between innovative form and traditional interior, and on the other from the magical illumination. Upon entering, the visitor is transported from the European world into the light of Japan. This aspect is genuinely connected to the meditative mood of the tea ceremony. One finds oneself instinctively following the course of the sun, rendered visible like beams by the internal system of ribbons, but also by the movement of the trees in the breeze. The darkening of the sky when rain is imminent is noticeable; the rain drops are audible as they would be on the roof of a traditional grass hut (*sō'an*). As night falls, the LED installation demonstrates its unforeseen power, although it illuminates the interior of the building only to a height of 1.5 m, leaving the ceiling vault relatively dark. In other words: the teahouse is entirely in keeping with the philosophy of traditional Japanese architecture, which provides a simultaneous quality of enclosure and transparency.

Kengo Kuma, who was born in Yokohama, Kaganawa Prefecture in 1954, is the Japanese architect who is most in tune with this philosophy. He studied at Tōkyō University and at Columbia University in New York. In 1987 he founded the Spatial Design Studio in Tōkyō, followed in 1990 by Kengo Kuma & Associates. His work has been awarded numerous national and international prizes. Today, Kengo Kuma creates architecture projects on three continents and teaches at the renowned Keiō University in Tōkyō. His oeuvre has been featured in numerous publications.[1]

Kengo Kuma: teahouse in the park of the Museum of Applied Arts Frankfurt. 2007
Kengo Kuma: Teehaus im Park des Museums für Angewandte Kunst Frankfurt. 2007

---

[1] The most comprehensive publications are Botond Bognar: Kengo Kuma — Selected Works. New York 2005. — Yukio Futagawa (ed.)/Kengo Kuma: Kengo Kuma (GA Architect 19), Tōkyō 2005.

und aufgeblasen. Nach 20 Minuten stand das Bauwerk und hatte nichts von dem visionären Charakter der ersten Computersimulationen verloren. Man hatte das Gefühl, dass es wie ein Lebewesen atmete. Dies war auch der Grund, warum sich der Begriff weak architecture gleichsam wie von selbst zu breathing architecture wandelte. Das Teehaus widerstand bereits am ersten Tage einem heftigen Gewittersturm, und bei dieser Gelegenheit konnte auch seine Lagerungsvorbereitung getestet werden. Die Membran darf keinesfalls nass entlüftet und gefaltet werden. So wurden Hülle und Luftpumpe vom Park des Museums in dessen Eingangshalle transportiert, wieder aufgeblasen und wo notwendig gereinigt. Nach etwa einer Stunde Trockenzeit konnte die Luft bis zum Vakuumzustand abgesaugt, die Hülle nach einem System gefaltet und dann zum Lagerort verbracht werden.

Nach dieser Vorbereitungsphase sowie der Anlage eines Teeweges mit 22 Granitstufen und zwei Brunnenschalen konnte die offizielle Einweihung des Teehauses am 18. August 2007 stattfinden. Mit wachsender Routine gelingt es dem vierköpfigen Aufbauteam heute, das Teehaus in zwei Stunden über der sauber gereinigten Bodenplatte aufzurichten, die *tatami*-Matten über einer Gummiisolierung auszulegen, die elektrische Feuerstelle zu installieren, den asymmetrischen Paravent aus Kyōto zu installieren und eine 300 Jahre alte Bambusvase in der größten Rundung des Gastraumes, die als *tokonoma*-Nische dient, zu befestigen. Hinter dem Paravent, der den Gastraum vom Vorbereitungsiglu trennt, befindet sich eine zweite Bodengrube, die alle Elektroinstallationen für den Teemeister beinhaltet. Die Teezeremonie kann beginnen.

2

Bemerkenswert am Teehaus Kengo Kumas ist dessen transzendentale Kraft, die zum einen aus dem Zusammenspiel von innovativer Form und traditioneller Einrichtung resultiert, zum anderen aus der zauberhaften Durchleuchtung. Der Besucher wird beim Eintritt der europäischen Welt entrückt und in das Licht Japans versetzt. Diese Möglichkeit ist genuin mit der meditativen Grundstimmung der Teezeremonie verbunden. Man folgt instinktiv dem Lauf der Sonne, die das interne Bändersystem wie Strahlen sichtbar werden lässt, aber auch die sich wiegenden Bäume. Die Verdunkelung des Himmels bei kommendem Regen ist spürbar, die Regentropfen sind wie auf dem Dach der traditionellen Grashütte (*sō'an*) hörbar. Und bei hereinbrechender Nacht entfaltet die LED-Anlage ihre ungeahnte Kraft, erleuchtet aber das Innere des Gebäudes nur auf 1,5 Meter Höhe, die innere Dachwölbung bleibt eher dunkel. Das Teehaus ist also ganz von der Philosophie traditioneller japanischer Architektur geprägt, die gleichzeitig Abschluss und Transparenz schenkt.

Kengo Kuma, der 1954 in Yokohama geboren wurde, ist der japanische Architekt, der dieser Philosophie am engsten verbunden ist. Sein Studium absolvierte er an der Tōkyō University und der Columbia University in New York. 1987 gründete er das Spatial Design Studio in Tōkyō, 1990 Kengo Kuma & Associates. Sein Schaffen wurde mit zahlreichen nationalen und internationalen Preisen gewürdigt. Kengo Kuma baut heute auf drei Kontinenten und lehrt an der renommierten Keiō University in Tōkyō. Über sein Werk sind zahlreiche Publikationen erschienen.[1]

---

[1] Die umfangreichsten Publikationen sind Botond Bognar: Kengo Kuma – Selected Works. New York 2005. – Yukio Futagawa (Hrsg.)/Kengo Kuma: Kengo Kuma (GA Architect 19), Tōkyō 2005.

In the design for the teahouse in the park of the Museum of Applied Arts Frankfurt, Kuma continues his practice of remembering the classic design principles and building philosophies of Japanese architecture. His architecture merges with nature, exemplified in the water/glass pavilion in Atami (1992-1995).[2] While the leitmotif in that building is the transient transparency of glass and sea, the basic shape of the teahouse is a reference to the rock islands in traditional Japanese stone gardens. At the same time, Kuma's creative lighting is intrinsically linked to the material of *shōji* paper, used, for example, as a timeless building material for the Takayanagi Community Centre in Kashiwazaki, Niigata (1998-2000).[3]

For the Frankfurt design, the architect chose Gore Tenara material, which he viewed as having the same aesthetic impact of allowing light to penetrate into the interior. Kuma has successfully experimented with the topic of transparency and innovative materials before. Examples are: the transparent walls of the Plastic House in Meguro (2000-2002)[4], the International Competition for Ephemeral Structures in Athens (2002)[5], the Oribe Teahouse, Tajimi, Gifu (2005)[6] and the EVA Project Kx K in the Hara Museum, Tōkyō (2005).[7] However, none of these examples have been as rigorous and lasting as the approach for the teahouse in Frankfurt.

What was the motivation that inspired Kengo Kuma and his team to undertake the extraordinary effort of implementing such a fleeting and mobile breathing architecture? No doubt it is underpinned by the desire to create a prototype in Europe which can then be utilized in Japan. Breathing architecture is an ideal solution for uses in Japanese cities, where soaring property costs mean that each unoccupied space translates into a loss. An inflatable structure for a few months, a restaurant, an exhibition space, these potentials are suddenly within reach of being realized — and all this within the template of a lifestyle culture, which breathes the fleeting life of nomads.

3

Ueno Park in the northern section of Tōkyō's downtown is one of the few large green spaces in the megalopolis. It has been accessible to the public since 1873 and is a popular destination for visits to the zoo, the national museums or the Tōshōgū Shrine. Every spring, tranquility turns to chaos when entire companies converge on the park with beer, *sake* and *karaoke* for a picnic under the thousands of cherry trees in the park to admire the annual spectacle of the blossoms.

Yet Ueno Park is also a magnet for the disadvantaged, those left stranded after having arrived at Ueno train station from the north and failing to find success in Tōkyō. In the past, one would see long-haired journeymen with tanned complexions, sleeping under bushes and doing little in the way of hygiene; the early 1990s saw the arrival of masses of young men from the Middle East, who started a lively trade in telephone cards.

In the mid-1990s the image changed. The entire parkland between zoo and museums became home to villages of bright blue plastic tents inhabited by hundreds if not thousands of men and also a few women. It may be that these people were refugees

Kengo Kuma: Water/Glass Pavilion, Atami, Shizuoka. 1992-1995
Kengo Kuma: Wasser/Glas-Pavillon, Atami, Shizuoka. 1992-1995

[2] Futagawa (see ftn. 1), pp. 24-31.
[3] Futagawa (see ftn. 1), pp. 86-89.
[4] Futagawa (see ftn. 1), pp. 112-115.
[5] Futagawa (see ftn. 1), p. 117.
[6] Futagawa (see ftn. 1), p. 196.
[7] Futagawa (see ftn. 1), p. 197.

Kengo Kuma: Oribe Teahouse. Tajimi, Gifu. 2005

Kengo Kuma: Oribe-Teehaus. Tajimi, Gifu. 2005

Beim Entwurf für das Teehaus im Park des Museums für Angewandte Kunst Frankfurt besinnt sich Kuma wie stets auf die klassischen Gestaltungsprinzipien und Baukunstphilosophien der japanischen Architekturen. Seine Architektur verschmilzt gleichsam mit der Natur, wie er es exemplarisch mit dem Wasser/Glas-Pavillon in Atami (1992-1995) zeigt.[2] Ist dort die flüchtige Transparenz von Glas und Meer das Leitmotiv, so weist bereits die Basisform des Teehauses auf die Umrisse der Felsinseln im traditionellen japanischen Steingarten. Gleichzeitig ist Kumas Beleuchtungskunst immanent mit dem Material des *shōji*-Papiers verbunden, das etwa als zeitloses Baumaterial beim Takayanagi Community Centre in Kashiwazaki, Niigata (1998-2000) verwendet wurde.[3]

Für den Frankfurter Entwurf verwendete er Gore-Tenara-Material, dessen ästhetische Wirkung des Lichteinfalls ihm gleichbedeutend erschien. Schon mehrfach hatte Kuma erfolgreich mit dem Thema der Transparenz und innovativen Materialien experimentiert, etwa bei den durchscheinenden Wänden des Plastic House in Meguro (2000–2002)[4], bei der International Competition for Ephemeral Structures in Athen (2002)[5], dem Oribe Tea house, Tajimi, Gifu (2005)[6] oder bei dem EVA Project KxK im Hara Museum, Tōkiō (2005)[7] – nie jedoch so konsequent und nachhaltig wie bei dem Frankfurter Teehaus.

Mit welchen Beweggründen aber haben Kengo Kuma und sein Team die erhebliche Anstrengung unternommen, solch eine flüchtige und mobile, atmende Architektur durchzusetzen? Sicher steht dahinter der Wunsch, in Europa ein Experiment zur Serienreife gelangen zu lassen, das in Japan

Homeless tent village, Ueno Park, Tōkyō. 1997

Obdachlosensiedlung, Ueno-Park, Tōkyō. 1997

Anwendung finden kann. Breathing Architecture ist in idealer Weise in japanischen Metropolen einzusetzen, wo enorme Grundstückskosten jeden Leerstand zum Verlust machen. Eine aufblasbare Architektur für einige Monate, ein Restaurant, eine Kunsthalle, das rückt nun in den Bereich der Realisierung – und dies alles vor der Folie einer Lifestyle-Kultur, die das flüchtige Leben der Nomaden atmet.

3

In der nördlichen Innenstadt Tōkiōs liegt mit dem Ueno-Park eine der wenigen großen Grünflächen der Megalopolis. Seit 1873 steht sie den Bürgern zur Verfügung, die sonntags wie werktags gerne den dortigen Zoo besuchen, die Nationalmuseen oder den Tōshōgū-Schrein. Alljährlich im Frühjahr bricht in diesem Park das Chaos aus, wenn unter den tausend Kirschbäumen ganze Firmen mit Bier, *Sake* und *Karaoke* zum Picknick und zur Bewunderung der Blüten zusammenkommen.

Doch der Ueno-Park war immer auch Anlaufpunkt für die Zukurzgekommenen, jene Gestrandeten, die aus dem Norden am Ueno-Bahnhof angekommen waren und in Tōkiō ihr Glück nicht gefunden hatten. Früher sah man langhaarige Gesellen mit brauner Haut, die unter den Büschen schliefen und wenig für ihre Sauberkeit taten; zu Beginn der 1990er Jahre kamen dann Massen von jungen Männern aus dem Mittleren Osten, die einen schwunghaften Handel mit Telefonkarten trieben.

Mitte der 1990er Jahre veränderte sich freilich das Bild. Auf dem gesamten Parkplateau zwischen Zoo und Museen entstanden Dörfer aus leuchtend blauen Plastikzelten, in denen Hunderte, wenn nicht Tausende von Männern und auch einige Frauen wohnten. Vielleicht waren diese Menschen auch auf der Flucht

[2] Futagawa (wie Anm. 1), S. 24-31.
[3] Futagawa (wie Anm. 1), S. 86-89.
[4] Futagawa (wie Anm. 1), S. 112-115.
[5] Futagawa (wie Anm. 1), S. 117.
[6] Futagawa (wie Anm. 1), S. 196.
[7] Futagawa (wie Anm. 1), S. 197.

fleeing from the enormous pressures to achieve success that marks Japanese society, victims of the *hikikomori* syndrome, in other words, individuals who felt compelled to run away from their families.[8] Clearly they pursued some kind of work during the day, for the improvised homes would stand empty then. In the evening, on the other hand, the villages were a beehive of social activity.

The structure of this settlement created by victims of the economic crisis at the time, whose last resort had become an existence as nomads in the megacity, was truly remarkable. Cleanliness and order must have been to them the last vestige of dignity, for everything was well organized, people looked after their hygiene, delicious aromas wafted from their cooking stations and they made use of the public washroom facilities in the park.

And how did the proud Tōkyō citizens deal with their cleanly vagabonds? They simply refused to acknowledge their existence. But on a summer day in 1998, the inhabitants of the village in the Ueno-Park were suddenly awoken. They had to disappear. The number of security personnel was unusually high and when questions were asked it turned out that a member of the imperial house was scheduled to visit the national museum on the other side. The prince must not be disturbed by a group on the margins of society. The visit to the museum was over by noon and the village dwellers of Ueno-Park, who had passed the time hidden away in side streets, returned with all their belongings strapped to bicycles and carts. Two hours later, the tents stood once again, all proper and tidy as if arranged by a ruler.

Living in fleeting buildings as an option in Asia? In tropical Calcutta with its chaotic life, shelters of this kind seem familiar. A small space in front of a store is rented by an organizer. During the day, all personal belongings are stored away, while a five-member family crowds into a niche next to the store, cooking and collecting water from a nearby hydrant. When the store closes a plastic sheet is stretched out between a light pole and a meter, and it is beneath this makeshift covering that people, animals and the sparse belongings are sheltered from the heavy rains.[9]

Although the building materials are the same as in the village in Ueno-Park described above, the people in Calcutta are settled only at night. The complete reorganization twice a day represents a completely different way of life. By comparison the weak architecture of the seemingly homeless people in Tōkyō is more reminiscent of yurt villages, still found, for example, in the autonomous region of Xinjiang. There, too, the structures are semistable units constructed from flexible materials, wood and felt, which are only left behind in certain seasons and for emergencies. All belongings have a fixed place within and remain there throughout.[10]

Japanese architects have been fascinated by such tendencies towards semimobile housing units since the 1980s. Thus Tōyō Itō created concepts for minimal and small housing units that were to be attached to or inserted into larger units with his Pao I and II: A Dwelling for Tōkyō Nomad Women from 1985 and 1989. His Nomad restaurant, conceived for very short-term uses, also

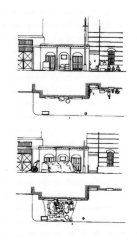

Street dwelling, Calcutta. 1990
Straßenbehausung, Kalkutta. 1990

---

[8] Wolfgang Harth/Andreas Hillert: "Lifestyle-Erkrankungen in der Dermatologie." In: Der Hautarzt, Vol. 58, No. 10, 2007, p. 864.

[9] Michael Bier: Asien: Straße, Haus — Eine typologische Sammlung asiatischer Wohnformen. Stuttgart 1990, pp. 48–49.

[10] Bier (see ftn. 9), pp. 52–53.

Yurts, Tianchi, Xinjiang. 1990
Jurten, Tianchi, Xinjiang. 1990

vor dem enormen Leistungsdruck der japanischen Gesellschaft, also Opfer des *hikikomori*-Syndroms, das sie vor ihren Familien flüchten ließ.[8] Offensichtlich gingen sie tagsüber einer Arbeit nach, denn die improvisierten Häuser waren verwaist. Am Abend herrschte jedoch reges soziales Leben.

Die Struktur dieser Siedlung von Opfern der damaligen Wirtschaftskrise, denen nur das Nomadendasein in der Großstadt geblieben war, war bemerkenswert. Sauberkeit und Ordnung bedeutete für sie wohl den letzten Rest von Würde, denn alles war wohlorganisiert, diese Menschen achteten auf Reinlichkeit, von ihren Kochstätten duftete es, und sie nutzten die öffentlichen Bedürfnisanstalten des Parks.
Wie gingen die stolzen Tōkiōter mit ihren reinlichen Loosern um? Sie nahmen sie schlichtweg nicht zur Kenntnis. Einzig an einem Sommertag im Jahre 1998 wurden die Einwohner des Dorfes im Ueno-Park aufgestört. Sie mussten verschwinden. Auf Nachfrage bei den ungewöhnlich zahlreich anwesenden Ordnungskräften stellte sich heraus, dass ein Mitglied des Kaiserhauses das Nationalmuseum gegenüber besuchen würde. Der Prinz sollte nicht durch eine soziale Randgruppe verstört werden. Mittags war der Museumsbesuch beendet, und die Dorfbewohner, die in den Seitenstraßen verharrt hatten, kehrten mit Sack und Pack, mit Rädern und Karren zurück. Zwei Stunden später standen die Planenhäuser wieder – wie mit der Richtschnur ausgezirkelt.

Das Leben in fliegenden Bauten, eine asiatische Möglichkeit? Im tropischen Kalkutta mit seinen chaotischen Lebensformen scheinen

solche Unterbringungen vertraut. Ein kleiner Platz vor einem Laden im Zentrum wird von einem Organisator gemietet. Tagsüber werden alle Habseligkeiten verpackt, und in einer Nische neben dem Laden hockt die fünfköpfige Familie, kocht und holt ihr Wasser von einem nahe gelegenen Hydranten. Nach Ladenschluss wird zwischen einem Lichtmasten und einem Zählerkasten eine Plastikfolie gespannt, unter der Menschen, Tiere und der wenige Besitz vor den heftigen Regengüssen Zuflucht finden.[9]

Zwar sind die Baumaterialien die gleichen wie bei dem beschriebenen Dorf im Ueno-Park, doch sind die Menschen in Kalkutta nur nachts sesshaft. Die zweifache Umrüstung jeden Tag stellt eine andere Lebensform dar. Die schwache Architektur der scheinbar wohnsitzlosen Tōkiōter gleicht dagegen eher den Jurtendörfern, wie sie etwa noch in der autonomen Region Xinjiang vorgefunden werden. Auch hier handelt es sich um semistabile Wohneinheiten in flexiblem Material, Holz und Filz, die nur saisonal oder in Notfällen verlassen werden. Aller Besitz hat seinen festen Platz und bleibt während des gesamten Aufenthaltes dort.[10]

Solche Tendenzen zu semimobilen Wohneinheiten faszinieren japanische Architekten seit den 80er Jahren. So schuf Tōyō Itō mit seinen Pao I and II: A Dwelling for Tōkyō Nomad Women 1985 und 1989 Konzepte für kleinste und kleine Wohneinheiten, die in größere Einheiten eingehängt oder eingeschoben werden sollten. Auch sein für sehr kurzfristige Nutzung konzipiertes Nomad Restaurant arbeitet auf 428 Quadratmetern mit flexiblen Elementen.[11] Diese Konzepte wurden mit Hilfe von kleinen, möglichst mobilen Container-

[8] Wolfgang Harth/Andreas Hillert. Lifestyle-Erkrankungen in der Dermatologie. In: Der Hautarzt, Bd. 58, Nr. 10, 2007, S. 864
[9] Michael Bier: Asien: Straße, Haus – Eine typologische Sammlung asiatischer Wohnformen. Stuttgart 1990, S. 48-49.
[10] Bier (wie Anm. 9), S. 52-53
[11] Tōyō Itō. Blurring Architecture. Ausst. Kat. Aachen, Antwerpen 1999/2000, S. 219-222.

functions with flexible elements covering a total area of 428 square meters.[11] These concepts were realized with the help of small, very mobile container units suited for transport. Riken Yamamoto used similar units in 1988 for his Hamlet Housing in Tōkyō, in which dwellings are supported by steel frames and covered by a tent roof.[12] Fashion also responded to the idea of nomad life in the city by creating nomad clothing. In 1992, Kosuke Tsumura, a former associate of Issey Miyake, presented his FINAL HOME coat. It features forty-four pockets and can serve as a shelter against the elements, for example if stuffed with leaves, should one have left one's home temporarily or permanently.

Mobile living, urban nomad life, is thus understood as a concept by architects and designers rather than a necessity and contrary to the example in the Ueno park. Japanese architect Shigeru Ban's reaction was completely different, naturally in part informed by the all too real loss of house and home after the Hanshin earthquake in Kōbe in 1995. Now he had an opportunity to put his otherwise rather ornamental material, the processed cardboard tube, to very practical use. He created block houses covered in tarps in an almost pretty way and propped up on top of sand-filled beer cases. Yet even for a comfortable lifestyle or leisure, the architect suggests houses that abandon too much solid material in favor of fabric or glass.[13]

4

In designing the teahouse for the Museum of Applied Arts Frankfurt, Kengo Kuma was thus able to build on concepts and practical experiments from the past three decades, as well as on traditional teahouse architecture, which aims to be ephemeral in nature by definition. The teahouse requires direct contact with the environment on the one hand, while removing the visitor from the same environment on the other. Moreover it is very lightweight in construction, since these structures do not feature the double-walled construction of *shōji* and *amado*. The visitor can hear and smell the surrounding garden and even catch a glimpse of it from time to time through a small grilled window.

The teahouse also transforms us, who work in Richard Meier's severe architecture that is nevertheless close to nature, into urban nomads on a smaller scale. When a tea master comes to visit, we carry the shell out onto the concrete foundation in good weather, roll the trunk that holds the pump into the park and let the teahouse unfold before our eyes like a blossom. Then the tea master can enact his or her performance. Sometimes, however, it is also a beautiful experience to simply sit in front of the teahouse and wait for evening and night to fall. Suddenly — and surprisingly — the teahouse takes on the appearance of a gleaming block of ice fallen from the outer space: breathing architecture with which one would enjoy wandering like a vagabond through a transcendent world.

Riken Yamamoto: Hamlet Housing. Tōkyō. 1988
Riken Yamamoto: Hamlet Housing. Tōkyō. 1988

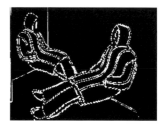

Kosuke Tsumura: FINAL HOME coat. 1992
Kosuke Tsumura: Mantel FINAL HOME. 1992

Shigeru Ban: emergency shelters, Kōbe. 1995
Shigeru Ban: Notunterkünfte, Kōbe. 1995

[11] Toyo Ito. Blurring Architecture. Exhibition catalog. Aachen/Antwerp 1999/2000, pp. 219-222.
[12] Toyo Ito (see ftn. 11), pp. 18-19. Francesco Montagna: Birkhäuser Architectural Guide Japan 20th Century, Basel 1997, p. 117.
[13] Shigeru Ban. Projects in Process to Japanese Pavilion, Expo 2000 Hanover. Exhibition catalog. Gallery MA Tōkyō 1999, pp. 58, 77, 79.

Shigeru Ban: Curtain House,
Tōkyō. 1995
Shigeru Ban: Curtain House,
Tōkyō. 1995

Kengo Kuma: Teahouse in the park of
the Museum of Applied Arts Frankfurt.
Elevation at night. 2007
Kengo Kuma: Teehaus im Park des
Museums für Angewandte Kunst Frankfurt.
Nachtansicht. 2007

einheiten umgesetzt, die transportabel sind.
Solche Einheiten verwendete zum Beispiel
Riken Yamamoto 1988 in seinem Tōkiōter
Hamlet Housing, bei dem Dwellings in
Stahlrahmen verspannt sind und von einem
Zeltdach überspannt werden.[12] Auch das
Modedesign kam der Idee des City-Nomaden-
tums mit Nomadenkleidung entgegen. 1992
stellte Kosuke Tsumura, ein ehemaliger
Mitarbeiter von Issey Miyake, seinen Mantel
FINAL HOME vor. Dieser weist 44 Taschen
auf und bietet, etwa mit Laub ausgestopft,
Schutz vor den Unbilden der Witterung,
wenn man sein Haus, sei es kurzfristig oder
für immer, verlassen hat.

Mobiles Wohnen, das städtische Nomadentum,
wird, anders als im Beispiel Ueno-Park, von
Architekten und Designern also eher als
Konzept denn als Notwendigkeit verstanden.
Ganz anders, freilich auch wegen des
realen Verlustes von Haus und Dach über
dem Kopf, reagierte der japanische Architekt
Shigeru Ban nach dem Hanshin-Erdbeben
in Kōbe 1995. Hier konnte er seinen sonst
eher ornamentalen Werkstoff, die nach-
behandelte Pappröhre, sehr nutzbringend
einsetzen. Er schuf Blockhäuser, die mit
Planen fast schmuck gedeckt waren und
auf sandgefüllte Bierkästen gebockt waren.

Aber auch für das komfortable Leben oder
für die Freizeit schlägt er Häuser vor, die
auf zu viel festes Material durchaus ver-
zichten und sich stattdessen mit Stoff oder
Glas behelfen.[13]

4

Beim Teehaus für das Museum für Angewandte
Kunst Frankfurt konnte Kengo Kuma also
auf Konzepten und praktischen Versuchen
der vergangenen drei Jahrzehnte aufbauen,
darüber hinaus auf der traditionellen Teehausarchitektur, die ja eher ephemerer Natur
sein will. Das Teehaus bedarf des direkten
Kontaktes mit der Umwelt einerseits, andererseits ist der Besucher dieser Umwelt entrückt.
Auch ist es sehr leicht gebaut, verzichtet
doch seine Architektur auf die Zweischalig-
keit von *shōji* und *amado*. Der Besucher
kann den umgebenden Garten hören und
riechen und gelegentlich durch ein kleines
Gitterfensterchen auch sehen.

Mit dem Teehaus werden auch wir, die wir
in der strengen und doch naturverbundenen
Architektur Richard Meiers arbeiten, ein
wenig zu Stadtnomaden. Haben wir Besuch
von einem Teemeister, so tragen wir bei
schönem Wetter die Hülle auf das Beton-
fundament, rollen die Pumpentruhe in den
Park und lassen das Teehaus sich entfalten
wie eine Blüte. Dann lassen wir den Teemeister
wirken. Manchmal ist es aber auch nur
schön, vor dem Teehaus zu sitzen und den
Abend, die Nacht zu erwarten. Plötzlich und
überraschend steht das Teehaus dann als
gleißender Eisblock wie aus dem All gefallen
da – breathing architecture, mit der man
durch eine transzendente Welt vagabundieren
möchte.

---

[12] Tōyō Itō (wie Anm. 11), S. 18-19. Francesco Montagna: Birkhäuser Architectural Guide Japan 20th Century,
Basel 1997, S. 117.
[13] Shigeru Ban. Projects in Process to Japanese Pavilion, Expo 2000 Hannover. Ausst. Kat. Gallery MA Tōkyō
1999, S. 58, 77, 79.

Volker Fischer

Designing with Air — Pneumatic Structures in Architecture,
Design, Art and Fashion

Mit Luft gestalten — pneumatische Konstruktionen
in Architektur, Design, Kunst und Mode

The flexible, heatable, double-walled white textile membrane of Kengo Kuma's teahouse in Frankfurt arises out of a long tradition of pneumatic-based designs. Moreover the teahouse is on such an intimate scale that inflatable design objects also come to mind as sources of inspiration. Pneumatic structures can be conceptually and physically realized thanks to viscose, elastic materials; in other words, rubber and plastics.

In 1852, the American Charles Goodyear invented inflatable automobile tires made from hard rubber, followed in 1888 by John Dunlop who developed the inflatable bicycle tire. Ever since their invention and to this day, these air-filled tires are referred to as "pneus." In the Greek "pneuma" means "breath," "exhalation" and, in a more figurative sense, an air-like, ethereal substance and "the spirit of god." These definitions give insight into the fact that inflation with air has lost none of its fascination to this day, since it is a kind of mimicry of the primary physical process of breathing in and out. "Breath" is the substance which transforms inanimate objects into animate creatures. Infusing the breath of life has played a continual role from the references in the bible to the Czech narrative of the Golem. This transfer of the breath of life continues to reverberate, whispering to us from all inflatable chairs, every air mattress, every balloon but also from every pneumatic architectural structure.

All biological cells, all organs and all living creatures, moreover, are derived from the "pneu." In the 1950s this fact was independently and systematically researched for the construction of lightweight structures

Die flexible, heizbare und doppelwandige Hülle aus weißem Textilstoff des Frankfurter Teehauses von Kengo Kuma steht in einer langen Tradition luftbasierter Gestaltungen. Das Teehaus ist zudem so intim dimensioniert, dass auch aufblasbare Designobjekte als Anregungspotenzial aufscheinen. Der mentale wie physische Kontext pneumatischer Konstruktionen wird durch viskoses, dehnungsfähiges Material, also Gummi und Kunststoffe, möglich.

1852 erfand der Amerikaner Charles Goodyear aufblasbare, aus Hartgummi hergestellte Autoreifen und 1888 John Dunlop den aufblasbaren Fahrradreifen. Aufgrund ihrer Luftfüllung heißen diese Reifen bis heute auch Pneus. Im Griechischen bedeutet „pneuma" so viel wie „Hauch", „Atem", aber im übertragenen Sinne auch luftartige, ätherische Substanz und „der Geist Gottes". Diese Bedeutungen verweisen auf die bis heute anhaltende Faszination von eingeblasener Luft, die ja den primären Körperprozess des Ein- und Ausatmens wiederholt. „Odem" ist jene Substanz, die aus unbelebten Gegenständen belebte Kreaturen macht. Die Lebenseinhauchung spielt von der Bibel an bis etwa zur Geschichte des tschechischen Golems eine kontinuierliche Rolle. Dieses Einhauchen von Leben schwingt noch mit, wispert uns aus allen aufblasbaren Sesselchen, aus jeder Luftmatratze, jedem Luftballon, aber auch aus jeder aufgeblasenen architektonischen Struktur entgegen.

Überhaupt entstehen ja alle biologischen Zellen, alle Organe und alle Lebewesen aus dem „Pneu". Dies haben in den 50er Jahren unabhängig voneinander Frei Otto in Deutschland und Walter Bird in den USA systematisch

by Frei Otto in Germany and Walter Bird in the United States.

Both, in turn, are in no small measure indebted to the geodesic domes of Buckminster Fuller, who, by the way, sketched out an "Air House" project of his own in 1959. In 1958 Frei Otto designed an air-supported pavilion for the Floriade agricultural show in Rotterdam and Bird founded Birdair Structures Inc., which soon grew into the world's leading manufacturer of air-supported structures. Over the course of the following decade, some 20,000 warehouses, athletic facilities, greenhouses and exhibition halls were realized as pneumatic structures in the United States, Germany, England, France and Japan. However, most of these were very fragile: in 1968 a single storm destroyed roughly 200 air-supported structures in northern Europe. The following statement remains nevertheless true: "The air-supported structure is one of the few truly fundamental innovations in building of the past one hundred years. It is doubtful whether in addition to tent, vault (incl. the shell) and post-and-beam construction, there can even be a comparable innovation for architecture."[1] It was only thanks to Frei Otto's research over many years that the air-supported structures became safer and more reliable.[2]

Parallel to the models in nature — organic bubbles, membranes, cells — there are a number of models in the field of alchemy. As early as 1957, when plastics were just taking off in the market place, Roland Barthes remarked that they were less a substance than the idea of the endless transformation of substance. Moreover, plastics are always associated with having a bad rap of being imitations. Yet this role of parvenu among materials is the very reason why this material

has proven so fascinating to antiauthoritarian pop culture since the 1960s: it is ephemeral, cheap and throwaway by definition. In the mid-1960s inflatables played a special role in the early urban happenings of Viennese avant-garde groups like Haus-Rucker-Co. and Coop Himmelb(l)au. Those inflatable, large-scale, transparent plastic spheres, whether suspended at great height in front of existing facades or being rolled through streets and squares, were always accessible and conceived as physiological/psychological extensions of human identity and experiential environments. The pneumatic "Villa Rosa" — a residential unit (1968) by Coop Himmelb(l)au — was a synesthetic bubble cosmos with color projections, sounds and scents for which the office created an urban complement in the same year with its "Cloud living unit" project. The raised temperatures in the interior, the perception of one's own body heat, the optic and visual distortion when looking onto the outside world, the warped acoustics — all this was intended to trigger an altered state and a most intensive self-awareness. This is especially true for the "Gelbes Herz" (Yellow Heart) pneumatic structure by Haus-Rucker-Co. (1968). It relates directly to breathing in and out and the very discourse of perception which Kengo Kuma now calls breathing architecture, for this Yellow Heart consisted of expanding and contracting air chambers. The (human) body and its vital function of breathing in and exhaling were translated into a theme as a synesthetic, realized art experience. In 1969 Coop Himmelb(l)au presented the "Herzraum Astroballon" in which the heartbeat was translated into a visible and audible pulsing light. As early as 1967, the Haus-Rucker-Co. group had

Haus-Rucker-Co.: "Gelbes Herz,"
Vienna 1968
Haus-Rucker-Co.: „Gelbes Herz",
Wien 1968

[1] Sabine Schanz: "Pneumatische Konstruktionen". In: Frei Otto, Bodo Rasch: Gestalt finden, Stuttgart 1995, p.114.
[2] Since 1958, Frei Otto and his Institute for Lightweight Structures in Stuttgart have carried out studies in engineering, mathematics and the natural sciences on the potential of ephemeral architectural concepts. Be it the German pavilion at the Expo in Montreal (1967), the Olympic Stadium in Munich (1968-72) or Shigeru Ban's Japanese pavilion at the Expo in Hanover (2000): none of these buildings would have been possible without Frei Otto's research.

Coop Himmelb(l)au: "Herzraum," 1969
Coop Himmelb(l)au: „Herzraum", 1969

für die Konstruktion von Lufthallen untersucht. Beide verdanken wiederum einiges den geodätischen Kuppeln Buckminster Fullers, der im Übrigen 1959 selbst ein Air House projektierte. 1958 plante Frei Otto einen luftgestützten Pavillon für die „Floriade" in Rotterdam, und Bird gründete die Firma Birdair, die bald zum weltweit führenden Hersteller von Lufthallen wurde. Im folgenden Jahrzehnt wurden in den USA, Deutschland, England, Frankreich und Japan etwa 20 000 Lagerhallen, Sportstätten, Gewächshäuser und Ausstellungshallen als pneumatische Konstruktionen errichtet. Die meisten von ihnen waren jedoch sehr fragil: So zerstörte 1968 ein einziger Sturm in Nordeuropa etwa 200 Lufthallen. Trotzdem bleibt richtig: „Die Lufthalle ist eine der ganz wenigen grundlegenden bautechnischen Neuerungen der letzten 100 Jahre. Es ist fraglich, ob es neben dem Zelt, dem Gewölbe (einschl. Schale) und der Stützen-Balken-Konstruktion überhaupt noch eine vergleichbare Innovation für das Bauwesen geben kann."[1] Erst durch Frei Ottos langjährige Forschungen konnten die Hallen sicherer werden.[2]

Aber neben der Ableitung aus der Natur – organische Blasen, Membranen, Zellen – stehen jene der Alchimie. Schon 1957 hatte Roland Barthes im Zusammenhang mit dem beginnenden Siegeszug der Kunststoffe bemerkt, dass diese allemal weniger eine Substanz als vielmehr die Idee ihrer endlosen Umwandlung seien. Zudem hafte dem Kunststoff immer der Geschmack des Imitats an. Diese Rolle aber, ein Parvenü der Materialien zu sein, ist der Grund für die Faszination, die dieses Material seit den 60er Jahren auf die antiautoritär eingestellte frühe Pop-Kultur ausübte: sein ephemerer Charakter, seine Billigkeit, seine Ex-und-

hopp-Anmutung. Mitte der 60er Jahre spielt Aufblasbares in diesem Kontext gerade in den frühen stadträumlichen Happenings der Wiener Avantgardegruppen wie Haus-Rucker-Co. und Coop Himmelb(l)au eine besondere Rolle. Jene aufblasbaren überdimensionalen durchsichtigen Kunststoffkugeln, ob in größerer Höhe vor existierende Fassaden gehängt oder durch die Straßen und Plätze von Städten gerollt, waren immer begehbar und als physio-psychische Erweiterungen der menschlichen Identität und Erfahrungskontexte gedacht. Die pneumatische Villa Rosa – eine Wohneinheit (1968) von Coop Himmelb(l)au – war ein synästhetischer Blasenkosmos mit Farbprojektionen, Tönen und Gerüchen, dem das Büro im gleichen Jahr mit seiner „Cloud living unit" urbanistische Dimensionen verlieh. Die im Inneren erhöhten Temperaturen, die Wahrnehmung der eigenen Körperwärme, die optischen und visuellen Verzerrungen beim Blick nach draußen, die veränderte Akustik – all dies sollte ein anderes Befinden und ein intensiveres Sich-selbst-bewusst-Werden auslösen. Dies gilt vor allem für die begehbare Pneu-Konstruktion „Gelbes Herz" (1968) von Haus-Rucker-Co. Sie bezieht sich unmittelbar auf das Ein- und Ausatmen und jenen Wahrnehmungsdiskurs, den Kengo Kuma heute breathing architecture nennt, denn dieses Gelbe Herz bestand aus sich ausdehnenden und zusammenziehenden Luftkammern. Der Körper selbst und seine Vitalfunktion des Ein- und Ausatmens wurde gewissermaßen als synästhetisches, entäußertes Kunsterlebnis thematisiert. 1969 präsentierte Coop Himmelb(l)au den Astroballon „Herzraum", in dem der Herzschlag sicht- und hörbar in pulsierendes Licht übersetzt wurde. Bereits 1967 hatte die Gruppe Haus-

[1] Sabine Schanz: „Pneumatische Konstruktionen". In: Frei Otto, Bodo Rasch: Gestalt finden, Stuttgart 1995, S.114.
[2] Frei Otto und sein Stuttgarter Institut für leichte Flächen-Tragwerke haben seit 1958 über Jahrzehnte hinweg die Möglichkeiten ephemerer Architekturkonzepte natur- und ingenieurwissenschaftlich untersucht. Weder der deutsche Pavillon der Weltausstellung in Montreal (1967) oder die Olympiabauten in München (1968-72) noch Shigeru Bans japanischer Pavillon auf der Expo in Hannover (2000) wären ohne Frei Ottos Forschungen möglich gewesen.

rolled large, transparent plastic spheres through the public spaces of Vienna: people could step inside and move them forward by walking. This project, called "Connection Skin", was not only an attempt at an almost psychedelic expansion of perception for the participants. It was also an early critical commentary on air pollution and a reference to oxygen as a limited resource. Coop Himmelb(l)au also rolled similar pneumatic psycho-spheres through Vienna and Basel in 1971. And at the Documenta V in Kassel in 1972, Haus-Rucker-Co. mounted a so-called "Oasis No. 7" in front of a second-floor window of the classicistic Fridericianum, furnishing it with plastic palm trees and a hammock: an ironic commentary on mass tourism dreams of exotic destinations but also an antiauthoritarian project because the transparent sphere in front of the classicistic facade took on the appearance of a chewing gum bubble stuck on the surface. The same Documenta also presented the fragile balloon structure of an oversized zeppelin by Belgian artist Panamarenko, albeit with one minor glitch: after the first few days Panamarenko's zeppelin deflated as air escaped, a fate similar to that of the large "Cubic feet package" by Christo — a 40,000 cubic meter air-filled plastic 'sausage' — which the artist had wanted to display as an open-air installation on the grounds of Documenta IV in 1966. Inflatable structures were quite ubiquitous in 1960s sculpture. As early as 1959 Piero Manzoni realized his "Corpi d'aria" followed one year later by the "Placentarium"; in 1966 Andy Warhol designed pneumatic "Clouds", Marinus Boezem created his "Air objects" and Hans Hollein installed colorful PVC sculptures in a park in Kepfenburg, Austria — Hollein, too, was a

member or at the very least a sympathizer of the architect/activists in Vienna. Pneumatic art has continued to the present day, for example Jeff Koons' "Inflatable Balloon Flower" (1997) or Takashi Murakami's manga-inspired, Mickey Mouse-like heads. The Haus-Rucker project "Live" (1970) in Vienna was also characterized by a protest against established values, dignified art forms and their idolization. The public itself was to become the exhibition object/subject, above all its trivial liveliness. Thus the center of the exhibition space features a glowing white air mattress, inflated to cover an area of 15 by 15 m, on top of which three glossy white spheres, each with a diameter of roughly 4 m, rolled about: as soon as people stepped into them, the visitors themselves were marginalized as objects within a giant billiards game. Taken as a whole, these urban supersymbols can be interpreted as psycho-physical blowups, a saturated form of pop art: ironic inquiries into the meaning of public space and the possibilities of participating in and with it. But inflatable structures have also been the subject of experimentation and implementation beyond Vienna. As early as 1965, the architect Arthur Quarmby realized an "Inflatable Dome" for Twentieth Century Fox in England, the Quasar group built an "Inflatable House" in 1968, and on the occasion of the World Fair in Osaka (1970), the United States pavilion, designed by Davis Brody, David Geiger and Walter Bird, as well as the Italian pavilion by architects De Pas, D'Urbino and Lomazzi consisted of pneumatic structures. At the same Expo, the Japanese architects Yutaka Murata and Mamoru Kawaguchi erected the Fuji pavilion, another inflatable pneumatic structure. The "Water Walk" project, presented

Haus-Rucker-Co.: "Oase Nr.7",
Kassel, 1972
Haus-Rucker-Co.: „Oase Nr.7",
Kassel, 1972

Christo: "Cubic feet package",
Kassel, 1966
Christo: „Cubic feet package",
Kassel, 1966

Jeff Koons: "Inflate Balloon Flower",
1997
Jeff Koons: „Inflate Balloon Flower",
1997

Takashi Murakami: "Untitled", 1997
Takashi Murakami: „Ohne Titel", 1997

Haus-Rucker-Co.: "Riesenbillard",
Vienna, 1970
Haus-Rucker-Co.: „Riesenbillard",
Wien, 1970

De Pas, D'Urbino, Lomazzi: Italian pavilion,
Expo Ōsaka, 1970
De Pas, D'Urbino, Lomazzi: Italienischer
Pavillon, Expo Ōsaka, 1970

Rucker-Co. große durchsichtige Kunststoff-kugeln durch den öffentlichen Raum der Stadt Wien gerollt, in die man einsteigen und die man durch Gehen vorwärtsbewegen konnte. Dieses „Connection Skin" genannte Projekt war nicht nur der Versuch einer für die Teilnehmer fast psychedelischen Wahrnehmungserweiterung, sondern zugleich auch ein früher kritischer Kommentar über Luftverschmutzung und ein Hinweis auf die Begrenztheit der Ressource Sauerstoff. Auch die Gruppe Coop Himmelb(l)au rollte solche pneumatische Psychoblasen 1971 durch Wien und Basel. 1972, auf der Documenta V in Kassel, montierte Haus-Rucker-Co. eine so genannte „Oase Nr. 7" vor ein Fenster im ersten Stock des klassizistischen Fridericianums und möblierte sie mit Plastikpalmen und Hängematte: einerseits ein ironischer Verweis auf die Träume des Massentourismus von Exotik, andererseits aber auch ein antiautoritäres Projekt, weil die durchsichtige Kugel vor der Klassizismus-fassade wie eine angeklebte Kaugummiblase wirkte. Auf der gleichen Documenta wurde die fragile Ballonkonstruktion eines über-dimensionierten Luftschiffes des belgischen Künstlers Panamarenko präsentiert, der allerdings ebenso nach den ersten paar Tagen die Luft ausging wie jenem großen „Cubic feet package", einer 40 000 Kubik-meter Luft fassenden Kunststoffwurst des Künstlers Christo, die dieser bereits 1966 auf der Documenta IV im Freien installieren lassen wollte. Überhaupt gab es in den 60er Jahren viele „inflatable structures" in der Bildenden Kunst.

Piero Manzoni realisierte bereits 1959 seine „Corpi d'aria" und ein Jahr später das „Placentarium", 1966 entwarf Andy Warhol pneumatische „Clouds", Marinus Boezem

seine „Air objects" sowie Hans Hollein bunte PVC-Skulpturen für den Park im österreichischen Kepfenburg – auch Hollein ein Mitglied oder zumindest Sympathisant der architektonischen Wiener Aktionisten. Bis in die Gegenwart hinein gibt es pneumatische Kunst, so etwa die „Inflatable Balloon Flower" (1997) von Jeff Koons oder die manga-affinen, mickeymausartigen Köpfe von Takashi Murakami.

Widerspruch gegen gesicherte Werte, würdevolle Formen der Kunst und ihre Beweihräucherung charakterisierte auch das Haus-Rucker-Projekt „Live" (1970) in Wien. Das Publikum selbst sollte zum Ausstellungsgegenstand werden, vor allem seine triviale Lebendigkeit. Und so befand sich im Zentrum des Ausstellungsraumes eine leuchtend weiße, 15 auf 15 Meter große aufgeblasene Luft-matte, auf der drei spiegelnd weiße Kugeln im Durchmesser von jeweils circa vier Metern herumrollten und nach dem Betreten die Menschen selbst zu Objekten eines Riesenbillards marginalisierten. Insgesamt können all diese urbanen Superzeichen als psycho-physische Blow-ups verstanden werden, gewissermaßen Pop-Art gesättigt: ironische Infragestellungen des öffentlichen Raumes und der Partizipationsmöglichkeiten in und an diesem. Aber nicht nur in Wien wurde mit Luftarchitekturen experimentiert und gearbeitet. So hatte bereits 1965 der Architekt Arthur Quarmby einen „Inflatable Dome" für das Filmunternehmen Twentieth Century Fox in England realisiert, die Gruppe Quasar konstruierte 1968 ein „Inflatable House", und auf der Weltausstellung in Ōsaka 1970 bestand der Landespavillon der USA, entworfen von Davis Brody, David Geiger und Walter Bird, ebenso wie der italienische Pavillon der Architekten De Pas, D'Urbino

in the same year by the British/Dutch Evenstructure Research Group consisted of a large, air-filled, transparent, three-dimensional and accessible PVC air sail, which literally enabled visitors to walk on water: once again a physiological and psychological expansion of human perception and senses and hence closely related to the aforementioned happenings by the Viennese groups.

"Structures gonflables" — the pivotal exhibition at the Paris Musée d'Art Moderne in March 1968 — provided the legitimizing, overarching cultural context for these antiauthoritarian, indeed anarchic and subversive activities in architecture and art, in fashion and design. The curators collected more than one hundred inflatable objects and complemented them with three designs of their own: a bubble house, a stadium and an exhibition hall.

A quarter of a century later, the pneumatic happenings of the 1960s matured into quasi realistic utopias. Festo, a German company, succeeded in 1999 with their "Pneuwing" airplane and one year later with the "Stingray II" test plane (first version 1998), which weighs in at a mere 80 kilo, has a wingspan of 13 meters and requires 60 cubic meters of air to take flight. These experimental planes were inspired, both aerodynamically and in terms of bionics, by Frei Otto's model studies of "Airfish" 1, 2, and 3 (1978, 1979, 1988). In 2005, Festo made explicit reference to Frei Otto's models when it released the "b-IONIC Airfish," albeit with both an ion beam drive and a plasma undulating drive. The future for both technologies lies chiefly in resistance reduction and resistance elimination. Naturally Festo, which specializes in

creating propulsion solutions for everyday applications, is also involved in the more conventional area of balloons in the tradition of Montgolfier's balloons (1783) filled with warm air or gas. The company became known primarily for a pneumatic exhibition hall, presented in 1997 under the name "Airtecture."

The most spectacular pneumatic architecture in recent years is, without a doubt, the Allianz-Arena stadium by Herzog & de Meuron in Munich, the external shell of which consists of gas-filled air chambers, which glow in red-white or blue-white depending on which team is playing, Bayern München or 1860 München.

A 12.5 m high "air cathedral" complete with pews, organ and stained-glass windows made of plastic developed in the Netherlands in 2004 is an inflatable, ironic hermaphrodite situated somewhere between architecture and product design. Congregations from some thirty countries have already expressed interest in the model. This pneumatic Gothic revival with enchantingly firm flying buttresses and priced at Euro 30,000, clearly belongs into the category of inflatable gimmicks, that is, ironic or self-mocking objects, which also include the 1.5 m high inflatable figure based on Edvard Munch's "The Scream," the most popular item in museum shops worldwide in 1998. The same shops, however, also sell a pneumatic Mona Lisa, a "Nana gonflable" based on the work by Niki de Saint-Phalle as well as inflatable Buddha figures, garden gnomes or space shuttles.

On a more serious note, there are inflatable chairs and stools by various renowned product designers. As early as 1960, a square

Yutaka Murata, Mamoru Kawaguchi: Fuji-Pavilion, Expo Ōsaka, 1970
Yutaka Murata, Mamoru Kawaguchi: Fuji-Pavillon, Expo Osaka, 1970

Quasar: "Inflatable House," 1968
Quasar: „Inflatable House", 1968

Festo: "Pneuwing," 1999
Festo: „Pneuwing", 1999

Festo: "Stingray," 1998
Festo: „Stingray", 1998

Air-cathedral, the Netherlands 2003
Luftkathedrale, Niederlande 2003

Inflatable figure based on Edvard
Munch's "The Scream," 1998
Aufblasfigur nach Edvard Munchs
„Der Schrei", 1998

und Lomazzi aus Pneu-Konstruktionen. Die japanischen Architekten Yutaka Murata und Mamoru Kawaguchi errichteten auf der nämlichen Expo den Fuji-Pavillon, ebenfalls als aufblasbare Pneu-Struktur. Das im gleichen Jahr vorgestellte Projekt „Water Walk" der britisch-niederländischen Gruppe Evenstructure Research Group bestand aus einem großen, luftgefüllten, transparenten, dreidimensionalen und begehbaren PVC-Luftsegel, mit dessen Hilfe man buchstäblich über den Wassern wandeln konnte: auch dies eine physio-psychische Erweiterung der menschlichen Befindlichkeiten und damit den erwähnten Aktionen der Wiener Gruppen nahe verwandt.

Den legitimierenden kulturellen Überbau zu diesen antiautoritären, durchaus anarchisch-subversiven Aktivitäten in der Architektur und Kunst, der Mode und dem Design lieferte die epochemachende Ausstellung „Structures gonflables" im Pariser Musée d'Art Moderne im März 1968. Die Kuratoren versammelten über 100 aufblasbare Objekte und ergänzten sie durch drei eigene Entwürfe eines Blasenhauses, eines Stadions und einer Ausstellungshalle.

Ein Vierteljahrhundert später dann pragmatisierten sich die Pneu-Happenings der 60er Jahre zu gewissermaßen realistischen Utopien. So reüssierte 1999 das deutsche Unternehmen Festo mit dem Flugzeug „Pneuwing" und ein Jahr später mit dem Versuchsflugzeug „Stingray II" (erste Version 1998), welches gerade einmal 80 Kilo wiegt, dreizehn Meter Spannweite hat und 60 Kubikmeter Luft benötigt, um fliegen zu können. Diese Versuchsflieger verdanken Frei Ottos Modellstudien „Airfish" 1, 2 und 3 (1978, 1979,

1988) ebenso aerodynamische wie bionische Anregungen. 2005 bezog sich Festo ausdrücklich auf Frei Ottos Modelle mit dem „b-IONIC Airfish", der nun allerdings ein Ionentriebwerk sowie einen Plasmawellenantrieb hat. Beide Technologien werden vor allem im Bereich der Widerstandsreduzierung von Strömungen zukünftig wichtig sein. Selbstverständlich engagiert sich Festo, im Alltag auf pneumatische Ventillösungen spezialisiert, auch im konventionelleren Bereich der Fesselballons, die auf die mit Warmluft oder Gas gefüllten Ballone von Montgolfier (1783) zurückgehen. Vor allem ist dieses Unternehmen durch eine pneumatische Ausstellungshalle bekannt geworden, die es 1997 unter dem Namen „Airtecture" vorstellte.
Die zweifellos spektakulärste Pneu-Architektur der letzten Jahre ist das Stadion der Allianz-Arena in München von Herzog & de Meuron, dessen Außenhülle aus gasgefüllten Luftkammern besteht, die je nach Belegung des Stadions durch Bayern München oder 1860 München in deren Farben Rot-Weiß oder Blau-Weiß erstrahlen können.

Ein aufblasbarer ironischer Zwitter zwischen Architektur und Produktdesign ist eine im Jahr 2003 in den Niederlanden entwickelte „Luftkathedrale" mit Sitzbänken, Orgel und Bleiglasfenstern aus Plastik von 12,5 Meter Höhe, an der bereits Kirchengemeinschaften aus rund 30 Ländern Interesse angemeldet haben. Diese Pneu-Neugotik für über 30 000 Euro mit allerliebsten prallen Strebepfeilern gehört eindeutig in den Bereich der aufblasbaren Gimmicks, also ironischer oder selbstironischer Objekte, zu denen auch die 1,50 Meter hohe, aufblasbare Figur nach Edvard Munchs „Der Schrei" zu zählen ist, die 1998 weltweit der Renner aller Museums-

stool made of transparent PVC, which Verner Panton had designed in 1954, went into production. It is divided into four chambers, which can be arranged at random and is also useable as a lounge chair. 1967 saw the arrival of a transparent variation of the Zanotta chair, called "Blow," by the architects De Pas, D'Urbino and Lomazzi: the closest thing to realizing Marcel Breuer's utopian dream of being able to one day sit down on a column of air. Having attained legitimacy through the success of the "Blow" chair, of which countless plagiarized versions exist today, the same three architects designed a transparent pedestrian tunnel in 1968, linking the two sections at the XIVth Triennial in Milan. The "Blow," like the "Sacco" bean bag by Gatti, Paolini and Teodoro, embodies the tendency to reinterpret fine furnishings as utilitarian furnishing, which began to overtake classic bourgeois ideas in the mid 1960s. The inflatable tables by Quasar (1967/69) and Fernando Campagna (1995) or the ironic "Sofina" air-seat variation (1999) of Le Corbusier's "LC2" chair by Joker (1999) also belong to the category of utilitarian furniture. Gaetano Pesce's "Up 5 Donna" chair, designed as far back as 1969, is another ironic piece of furniture. Compressed to one-tenth of its volume, this foam chair only unfolds to its full size and erotomanic form after it has been unpacked. Ron Arad's "Transformer Chair" from 1981, a PVC piece containing polyester granulate, is wrapped in a high-tech cloak and was probably created out of a conscious nostalgia for the 1960s. When air is extracted from this chair with a vacuum cleaner, the granulate automatically assumes the form left behind by the last impression of a body seated in the chair — last but not least an

ironic paraphrase of the famous "Sacco" bean bag. Arresting a body position in a moment in time always has something magical, even alchemical about it. Conversely, the "Pisolo" air bed and the "Pistola" chair by Denis Santachiara (both 1999) are characterized by the joy found in surprising combinations: a stool can be blown up into a bed, simultaneously generating a side table. And finally in 2006, the Swiss company Wogg introduced the "Air Chair" to a market, a comfortable lounge chair filled to bursting with air.

Yet these utopias and alternative forms of living, and also the joy in aesthetic and even scientific experimentation which distinguishes the inflatable architecture and furniture of the 1960s are only present today in the form of revival. Standard contemporary fun and lifestyle products have very little in common with the anti-authoritarian, anti-bourgeois attitude of that era. Contemporary examples include Mike Hoppe's thirty "Embargo" sofas and chairs as well as the Christmas trees and fruit objects, flowers and cactus lamps by Korean designer Shiu-Kay Kan, whose SKK label has propelled him to become the worldwide leader in the market for inflatable objects. From his base in London, Shiu-Kay Kan delivers inflatable cactus lamps, Christmas trees, illuminated ghosts, sunflowers, orchids and backpacks to over 2,000 stores. The Swiss enterprise Klang & Kleid has also joined the party in this sector.
Another London-based company, albeit far more respectable, is the design office Inflate: although dabbling in fun products from time to time, the principal objective of the office is to create products as serious

Inflatable buddha "Silly," 2001
Aufblasbarer Buddha „Silly", 2001

Festo: "Airtecture," 1997
Festo: „Airtecture", 1997

Gaetano Pesce: "Up 5 Donna" chair, 1969
Gaetano Pesce: Sessel „Up 5 Donna", 1969

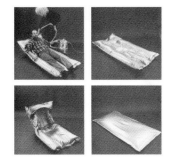

Ron Arad: "Transformer" chair, 1981
Ron Arad: Sessel „Transformer", 1981

Fernando Campagna: inflatable table, 1995
Fernando Campagna: Aufblasbarer Tisch, 1995

Nick Crosbie, Inflate: fruit basket, 1995
Nick Crosbie, Inflate: Obstkorb, 1995

shops war. Dort allerdings gibt es auch eine Pneu-Mona-Lisa, eine „Nana gonflable" nach Niki de Saint-Phalle sowie aufblasbare Buddhas, Gartenzwerge oder Space Shuttles.

Ernsthafter sind da die aufblasbaren Sitzgelegenheiten verschiedener arrivierter Produktentwerfer. Bereits 1960 ging ein querrechteckiger Hocker aus transparenter Kunststoff-Folie von Verner Panton in die Produktion, der schon 1954 entworfen worden war. Er ist in vier Kammern unterteilt, beliebig aneinanderzureihen und auch als Liege verwendbar. 1967 kommt vor allem die durchsichtige Variante des Zanotta-Sessels „Blow" der Architekten De Pas, D'Urbino und Lomazzi dem utopischen Traum Marcel Breuers ziemlich nahe, der davon schwärmte, dereinst tatsächlich auf einer Säule von Luft Platz nehmen zu können. Vom Erfolg des „Blow"-Sessels legitimiert, den es bis heute in unzähligen Plagiaten gibt, entwarfen diese drei Architekten 1968 einen transparenten Fußgängertunnel, der die beiden Abteilungen der XIV. Mailänder Triennale verband. Der „Blow" steht ebenso wie der Sitzsack „Sacco" von Gatti, Paolini und Teodoro für die Tendenz der Umwertung von hochwertigen Gebrauchsmöbeln zu Verbrauchsmöbeln, die Mitte der 60er Jahre klassisch bürgerliche Vorstellungen ablösten. Ebenso gehören der aufblasbare Tisch von Quasar (1967/69) und Fernando Campagna (1995) oder die ironische Luftsitz-Variante „Sofina" (1999) des Unternehmens Joker (1999) des Le Corbusier-Sessels „LC 2" in den Kontext von Verbrauchsmöbeln. Auch Gaetano Pesces Sessel „Up 5 Donna", bereits 1969 entworfen, ist ein ironisches Möbel. Auf ein Zehntel seines Volumens zusammengedrückt, entfaltete dieses Schaumstoffmöbel seine eigentliche Größe und erotomane Form

erst nach dem Auspacken. Im Hightech-Gewand kommt uns jener 1981 wahrscheinlich durchaus in bewusster Nostalgie an die 60er Jahre entstandene „Transformer-Sessel" von Ron Arad entgegen, der aus PVC besteht, aber Polysterolgranulat enthält. Wenn mit einem Staubsauger diesem Sitz Luft entzogen wird, gruppiert sich das Granulat als Körperabdruck jener Sitzhaltung, die zuletzt eingenommen wurde — nicht zuletzt eine ironische Paraphrase auf den berühmten Sitzsack „Sacco". Das Einfrieren von Körperpositionen hat immer etwas Magisches, ja Alchimistisches. Dagegen kennzeichnen das Luftbett „Pisolo" und den Sessel „Pistola" von Denis Santachiara (beide 1999) eher die Freude an den Überraschungen der Kombinatorik: Ein Hocker lässt sich zum veritablen Bett aufpusten und generiert solchermaßen den Beistelltisch gleich mit. 2006 schließlich stellte das Schweizer Unternehmen Wogg den aufblasbaren Sessel „Air Chair" vor, eine prall-bequeme Lounge-Liege.

Aber jene Utopien und alternative Wohnformen, jene Freude auch am gestalterischen, ja wissenschaftlichen Experiment, die die Pneu-Architekturen und -Möbel der 60er Jahre auszeichnet, werden heute nur noch als Revival-Produkte wiederbelebt. Die gegenwärtigen einschlägigen Fun- und Lifestyle-Produkte haben mit jenem antiautoritären, antibürgerlichen Gestus nur noch sehr lose zu tun. Dazu gehören die etwa 30 „Embargo"-Sofas und -Sessel von Mike Hoppe ebenso wie Christbäume und Obstobjekte, Blumen und Kaktusleuchten des koreanischen Designers Shiu-Kay Kan, der mit seinem Label SKK weltweit Marktführer in diesem Luftnummer-Segment ist. Er beliefert von London aus mehr als 2000 Geschäfte mit

industrial design. The designers of this group — Nick Crosbie, Marc and Michael Sodeau as well as Nitzan Yaniv — also employ PVC and high-frequency welding techniques to produce their colorful plastic objects for affordable prices, including inflatable fruit baskets, egg cups, picture frames, spectacle display cases or invitation cards. From the mid-1990s onward, the Inflate designers have increasingly worked on large fair presentations, room dividers or more complex installations for product campaigns. APA, a German enterprise, also operates in this sector of product placement, marketing all kinds of inflatables from 6 m high X-Boxes for Microsoft to a truck-size computer mouse.

At any rate, inflatable objects, be it for private or public uses, are attractive because they can be efficiently and easily stored once they are deflated. These are temporary products, so to speak, which are activated to usage status only when they are truly needed. It is reasonable to remark, therefore, that such inflatables have redefined the landscape of the home as a place without conventional furnishings as well as some areas in the public sphere since the mid-1960s.

All symbolic-iconographic and societal implications of an anti-authoritarian «lightness of being» as well as increased mobility aside, another important factor is the inexpensive production of such objects, which applies not only to cushions, flowers or chairs, but also to voluminous sofas, even cabinets and room dividers. Towards the end of the 1990s, the Inflate designer Nick Crosbie stated in a beautifully disarming fashion that: "The acquisition of the high-frequency welding tool was the best investment I've ever made.

[...] We aren't interested in all the ballast that goes along with the ownership and operation of a manufacturing plant. On the other hand, we do have our own machines for manufacturing prototypes and limited editions. [...] Working on inflatables is akin to a combination of geometry and couture. We hardly work with computers. I prefer to use a ruler, pencil, paper, knife, cardboard remnants and bit of twine. [...] For smaller objects you rely on the fact that the material creates the form as a result of its elasticity. Larger, architectonically conceived objects make it necessary to literally map the surface and design a cutting pattern."[3] Just such a cutting pattern was absolutely essential for Kengo Kuma's teahouse presented in this volume, especially since it is a prototype as is evident when reading the other contributions.

In addition to the examples culled from performance art and furnishings, the success of inflatables is manifest in other, far more functional contexts: not only car tires, air mattresses, balloons, hood-type hair-driers in salons and at home, but also so-called bio-balls as ergonomically healthier forms of seating in offices and inflatable casts for arm and leg fractures. This more specifically functional context also includes the options of lifting and moving existing structures by means of inflatable transportation mattresses: a solution that has already been put to use in the case of the historic Hotel Adlon from the Foundation Period, which had to be moved in the context of new development on Potsdamer Platz in Berlin and also for an older building in Moscow, which had to be shifted by 20 meters when a road was reconfigured.

Nick Crosbie, Inflate: "Screen" room divider, 1997
Nick Crosbie, Inflate: Paravent „Screen", 1997

Nick Crosbie, Inflate: "Signal" chair, 1997
Nick Crosbie, Inflate: Sessel „Signal", 1997

De Pas, D'Urbino, Lomazzi:
"Blow" chair, 1967
De Pas, D'Urbino, Lomazzi:
Sessel „Blow", 1967

[3] Nick Crosbie, in: Swell: inflate, Frankfurt 1998, no page.

Display for Microsoft's X-Box, APA
advertising campaign 2007
Display für die X-Box von Microsoft,
APA-Werbemittel 2007

"Nana gonflable" after Niki de
Saint-Phalle, 1998
„Nana gonflable" nach Niki de
Saint-Phalle, 1998

Evenstructure Research Group:
PVC-air sail "Waterwalk", 1968
Evenstructure Research Group:
PVC-Luftsegel „Waterwalk" , 1968

luftgestützten Kaktusleuchten, Weihnachts-
bäumen, Geisterlichtern, Sonnenblumen,
Orchideen und Rucksäcken. Auch das Schweizer
Unternehmen Klang & Kleid tummelt sich in
diesem Sektor.

Ebenfalls in London ansässig ist das wesentlich
seriösere Designbüro Inflate, welches sich
zwar gelegentlich auch mit Fun-Produkten
beschäftigt, aber dessen prinzipieller Anspruch
darin besteht, sich im Bereich des ernst-
haften Industriedesigns zu bewegen. Die
Designer der Gruppe, Nick Crosbie, Marc
und Michael Sodeau sowie Nitzan Yaniv,
benutzen ebenfalls PVC und Hochfrequenz-
Schweißtechniken, um ihre farbenfrohen
Plastikobjekte zu erschwinglichen Preisen
herzustellen, zu denen aufblasbare Obstkörbe,
Eierbecher, Bilderrahmen, Brillendisplays
oder Einladungskarten gehören. Ab Mitte der
90er Jahre produzierten die Inflate-Designer
zunehmend auch große Messepräsentationen,
Raumteiler oder komplexere Szenarien für
Produktkampagnen. Im Bereich dieses
Product Placement agiert auch das deutsche
Unternehmen APA, welches von sechs Meter
hohen X-Boxen bis zu lastwagengroßen
Computermäusen allerlei Inflatables in Ballon-
form auf den Markt bringt.

Überhaupt sind die aufblasbaren Gegenstände,
ob im privaten oder im öffentlichen
Zusammenhang, nicht zuletzt deshalb attraktiv,
weil sie nach dem Luftablassen problemlos
und platzsparend verstaut werden können.
Es sind gewissermaßen Produkte auf Zeit,
die nur dann in ihren Benutzungszustand
gebracht werden, wenn sie wirklich gebraucht
werden. Insofern ist festzuhalten, dass
solche Pneu-Produkte sowohl die Landschaft
des Heims als einen Ort ohne konventionelles

Mobiliar wie auch manche Bereiche im
öffentlichen Raum seit Mitte der 60er Jahre
neu definiert haben.
Aber neben allen symbolisch-ikonografischen
wie gesellschaftlichen Implikationen einer
antiautoritären „Leichtigkeit des Seins"
sowie einer erhöhten Mobilität ist vor allem
die kostengünstige Produktion solcher
Objekte wichtig, die ja nicht nur Kissen,
Blumen oder Sessel betrifft, sondern auch
volumige Sofas, sogar Schränke oder
Raumteiler. Ende der 90er Jahre formulierte
der Inflate-Designer Nick Crosbie mit
schöner Offenheit: „Die Anschaffung des
Hochfrequenz-Schweißgeräts war die beste
Investition, die ich je getätigt habe. [...]
Wir sind nicht scharf auf all den Ballast, der
zum Besitz und Betrieb einer Produktions-
anlage gehört. Allerdings haben wir unsere
eigenen Maschinen zur Herstellung von
Prototypen und Kleinserien. [...] Die Arbeit
an aufblasbaren Objekten ist so etwas wie
eine Mischung aus Geometrie und Damenschneiderei. Wir arbeiten kaum mit Computern.
Ich benutze lieber Lineal, Bleistift, Papier,
Messer, Pappreste und ein bisschen Bind-
faden. [...] Bei kleineren Objekten verlässt
man sich darauf, dass das Material aufgrund
seiner Dehnbarkeit die Form bildet. Größere,
architektonisch konzipierte Objekte machen
es notwendig, dass man die Oberfläche
buchstäblich kartografiert und ein Schnittmuster
entwirft."[3] Ein solches Schnittmuster war
auch, zumal es sich um einen erstmals
hergestellten Prototyp handelt, bei dem in
diesem Band in Rede stehenden Teehaus
von Kengo Kuma unerlässlich, wie aus anderen
Beiträgen hervorgeht.
Zum Erfolg von aufblasbaren Formen gehören
neben den Beispielen aus der Aktionskunst
und dem Mobiliar allerdings weitere, weitaus

[3] Nick Crosbie, in: Swell: inflate, Frankfurt 1998, o. S.

Every now and then inflatable dresses would appear in the world of haute couture, by Issey Miyake, for example, or Yoshi Yamamoto, Karl Lagerfeld, Sonia Rykiel, Jean Paul Gaultier, JC de Castelbajac and Moschino. This, too, is connected to the blend of geometry and couture described by Nick Crosbie, which Christina Morozzi describes as "hybrid, transparent-spatial expansions of the body" with a quality that is both erotic and masochistic: displayed, celebrated but untouchable.[4]

Issey Miyake: winter collection 2000/01
Issey Miyake: Winterkollektion 2000/01

Airbags installed in cars are more specifically high-tech products: ergonomically cleverly designed balloon creations, they fail to fully eliminate the risk of injury in accidents and, as seen in popular motion pictures, the activation of this mechanism can lead to strange limitations in mobility. The same may be true for the special inflatable Wonderbra, an image of which the "Bild"-Zeitung published at the beginning of 2001 next to a small, cute air pump. Evacuation slides and floating islands as emergency buffer zones used by airlines fall into the same category. One functioning airbag, incidentally, was an inflatable plastic cone originally developed by the Frankfurt design group Ginbande for a competition held by the champagne company Mumm as a champagne cooler. Designer Martin Ruiz de Azua, whose "Basic-House" (1999) unfolds from a wearable T-shirt into an inflatable cube to provide shelter from the elements, thinks on a larger scale.

Issey Miyake: winter collection 2000/01
Issey Miyake: Winterkollektion 2000/01

Generally speaking, the act of inflating, that is the continual increase of volume, also signifies a metaphor for design processes in principle. Ultimately its attractiveness lies in the opposite trend, the miniaturization of technological building blocks and electronics, whose volume has diminished to the point of being less than visible in the past fifteen to twenty years. Cell phones or MP3 players have now been reduced to the size of pieces of jewelry and are indeed often worn like necklaces. Conversely, the so-called "Blow Up" was a popular design strategy in the context of pop art. Shrinking and expanding are therefore clearly design parameters which reflect and utilize both the symbolism and attractiveness of continual change. This brings us back to the primary function of breathing in and exhaling. The ubiquity of this idea has periodically captivated all pragmatic three-dimensional design disciplines over the course of the twentieth century: from urban design and houses, from the art happenings by the Viennese performance artists and some haute couture designs all the way down to home accessories, furniture and fun objects.

Plastics on the whole and with them inflatables are characterized by a fascination that other materials do not engender. "Fundamentally, plastics are a spectacle that has to be deciphered: a spectacle of its ultimate results," Roland Barthes states and continues: "In the case of plastic, material unremittingly presents itself as a puzzle to the mind." Above all, however, Barthes emphasizes: "Plastic is the first magical material that is willing to assume ordinariness. For the first time, artificiality is intent on being ordinary rather than extraordinary."[5]

Yoshji Yamamoto: inflatable skirt, 1999
Yoshji Yamamoto: aufblasbarer Rock, 1999

In the case of Kengo Kuma's teahouse, however, the artificial has been fused with the habitual an inimitable way. This is a product of the high artistry and tremendously traditional Japanese tea ceremony itself,

[4] Christina Morozzi, in: Lux. Transparenza. Transparency (Lux 5), Marcon, Italy 2007, pp. 18 ff.
[5] Translated from Roland Barthes: "Plastik", in: Mythen des Alltags, Frankfurt 1964, p.79 ff. (original French edition "Mythologies", Paris 1957)

Sonia Rykiel: prêt-à-porter collection
1996
Sonia Rykiel: Prêt-à-porter- Kollektion
1996

Jean Paul Gaultier: winter collection
1995/96
Jean Paul Gaultier: Winterkollektion
1995/96

Martin Ruiz de Azua: "Basic House", 1999
Martin Ruiz de Azua: „Basic House", 1999

funktionalistischere Kontexte: nicht nur Autoreifen, Luftmatratzen, Luftballons, Haarhauben in Frisörsalons oder im Privathaushalt, sondern auch so genannte Biobälle zum ergonomisch gesünderen Sitzen im Büro sowie aufblasbare Bruchschienen für Arm- und Beinfrakturen. Und zu diesem engeren funktionalistischen Zusammenhang ist auch die Möglichkeit zu zählen, mit Druckluft vorhandene Häuser durch entsprechende Gleitmatratzen zu unterfüttern und dann zu verschieben: Dies geschah bei dem gründerzeitlichen Hotel Adlon im Zusammenhang mit der Neubebauung des Potsdamer Platzes in Berlin ebenso wie bei einem älteren Gebäude in Moskau, welches wegen einer neuen Straßenführung um 20 Meter versetzt werden musste.

In der Haute Couture gab es ab und zu aufblasbare Kleider, so etwa von Issey Miyake, Yoshi Yamamoto, Karl Lagerfeld, Sonia Rykiel, Jean Paul Gaultier, JC de Castelbajac oder Moschino. Auch das gehört zur von Nick Crosbie beschriebenen Mischung aus Geometrie und Damenschneiderei, die Christina Morozzi als „hybride, transparent-räumliche Erweiterungen des Körpers" mit zugleich erotischer wie masochistischer Qualität beschreibt: ausgestellt, angepriesen, aber unerreichbar.[4]

Dem engeren Bereich des Hightech sind die Airbags der Automobile zuzurechnen, ergonomisch ausgefuchste Ballonkreationen, auch wenn sie die Verletzungsgefahr bei Unfällen nicht vollständig beseitigen und, wie einschlägige Spielfilme zeigen, die Auslösung dieses Mechanismus merkwürdige Einschränkungen des Bewegungsapparates zur Folge haben kann. Dies mag auch jenen speziellen, aufblasbaren Wonderbra-Büstenhalter charakterisieren, dessen Bild nebst einer kleinen, niedlichen Luftpumpe Anfang 2001 die „Bild-Zeitung" publizierte. Und hierher gehören natürlich auch die Rettungsrutschen und Schwimminseln der Fluggesellschaften als abrufbare Pufferzonen geformter Luft. Ein funktionierender Airbag übrigens war auch ein aufblasbarer Kunststoffkonus, den die Frankfurter Designergruppe Ginbande für einen Designwettbewerb des Sektunternehmens Mumm als Sektkühler entwickelt hat. In größeren Dimensionen dagegen denkt der Entwerfer Martin Ruiz de Azua, dessen Basic-House (1999) sich aus einem tragbaren T-Shirt entfaltet und als aufblasbarer Würfel Schutz vor Wind und Wetter bieten soll.

Insgesamt allerdings bedeutet das Aufblasen, also die kontinuierliche Volumenvergrößerung, auch eine prinzipielle Metapher für Design- und Entwurfsprozesse überhaupt. Ihre Attraktivität gewinnt sie nicht zuletzt durch ihr Gegenteil, die Miniaturisierung technischer Baugruppen und elektronischer Geräte, deren Volumen sich seit 15, 20 Jahren bis hin zur Subvisualität verringert. Handys oder MP3-Player haben inzwischen die Größe von Schmuckstücken und werden gerne auch an einer Kette um den Hals getragen. Umgekehrt war das so genannte Blow Up im Kontext der Pop Art eine beliebte Entwurfsstrategie. Sowohl Schrumpfen wie Vergrößern sind also offenbar Entwurfsparameter, die die Symbolik und die Attraktivität von kontinuierlichen Veränderungen reflektieren und nutzen. Damit sind wir wieder bei der primären Lebensverrichtung des Ein- und Ausatmens angelangt. Die Ubiquität dieser Vorstellung hat im 20. Jahrhundert alle pragmatisch-dreidimensionalen Entwurfs-

---

[4] Christina Morozzi, in: Lux. Transparenza. Transparency (Lux 5), Marcon, Italien 2007, S. 18 ff.

informed by rituals that have evolved over centuries, but also by the unusual form of this inflatable teahouse itself, which is reminiscent to a double golf ball or a peanut to some visitors. The technological complexity is extraordinary and required intensive engineers' calculations and research. And it is all the more fascinating precisely because such technological complexity has in the end resulted in a light, intimate small building that is downright ephemeral in expression. Although this teahouse is no doubt at home in the pop-cultural domains of utopia and science fiction, perhaps even space exploration, Barbarella-like leisure behavior or the communication orgies of the British Archigram architects, it also exudes something that is uniquely distinctive: the flair and aura of contemplation as well as a fundamental context-driven modesty that is typical of this architect. Kengo Kuma always builds ephemeral manifestos, all the more visionary for their skillful nonchalance.

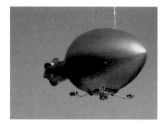

Frei Otto: „Airfish 2", 1979
Frei Otto: „Airfish 2", 1979

Air-cathedral, the Netherlands 2003,
wedding ceremony
Luftkathedrale, Niederlande 2003,
Trauzeremonie

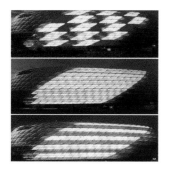

Herzog & de Meuron: "Allianz"-Arena,
Munich 2006
Herzog & de Meuron: „Allianz"-Arena,
München 2006

disziplinen immer wieder periodisch erfasst: von der Stadtplanung und den Häusern, von den Kunstaktionen der Wiener Aktionisten und manchen Entwürfen von Couturiers bis zu den Wohnaccessoires, Möbeln und Spaßutensilien.

Kunststoff überhaupt und damit auch die aufblasbaren Inflatables charakterisiert eine generelle Faszination, die andere Materialien so nicht haben. „Im Grunde ist das Plastik ein Spectaculum, das entziffert werden muss: das Spektakulum seiner Endergebnisse", sagt Roland Barthes und fährt fort: „Beim Kunststoff stellt sich die Materie dem Geist unablässig als ein Bilderrätsel dar." Vor allem aber betont er: „Kunststoff ist die erste magische Materie, die zur Alltäglichkeit bereit ist. Zum ersten Mal hat es das Artifizielle auf das Gewöhnliche und nicht auf das Seltene abgesehen."[5]
Im Falle des Teehauses von Kengo Kuma allerdings ist das Artifizielle mit dem Gewöhnlichen auf eine unnachahmliche Weise verschränkt. Dies hat einerseits mit der hohen, von großer Traditionalität geprägten Zeremonie des japanischen Teetrinkens zu tun, dessen Rituale sich über Jahrhunderte entwickelt

haben, andererseits aber eben auch mit der ungewöhnlichen Form dieses aufblasbaren Teehauses, das manche Beobachter an einen doppelten Golfball erinnert. Dabei ist die technische Komplexität außergewöhnlich hoch und erforderte intensivste ingenieurwissenschaftliche Berechnungen und Forschungen. Aber gerade weil aus einer solchen technischen Komplexität schließlich ein leichtes, geradezu ephemer wirkendes, intimes kleines Bauwerk entstanden ist, entfaltet sich dessen Faszination umso mehr. Zwar partizipiert dieses Teehaus durchaus an popkulturellen Bedeutungsfeldern der Utopie und der Science-Fiction, vielleicht sogar der Weltraumabenteuer, dem Leisuretime-Verhalten von Barbarella und den Kommunikativitätsräuschen der Stadträume der britischen Archigram-Architekten, aber hinzu kommt etwas entscheidend anderes: nämlich das Flair und die Aura von Kontemplation sowie jene für diesen Architekten typische Haltung einer prinzipiell kontextkompatiblen Bescheidenheit. Kengo Kuma baut eigentlich immer ephemere Manifeste, deren gekonnte Beiläufigkeit umso visionärer ist.

[5] Roland Barthes: „Plastik", in: Mythen des Alltags, Frankfurt 1964, S.79 ff.
(franz.Originalausgabe „Mythologies", Paris 1957)

Takumi Saikawa
Japanese and German Sense of Space
Japanisches und deutsches Raumgefühl

Study model No. 4, Sept. 2005

The teahouse looks like a peanut shell, golf ball, or a character in a Japanese anime. A friend, to whom I showed a photograph of the structure, said it was reminiscent of a large caterpillar. In the interior one has a sense being suspended in a light expanse, a strange feeling of weightlessness and a keen awareness of the position of the sun and the changing brightness. At night, the teahouse ressembles an overdimensioned light sphere.

Kengo Kuma was commissioned to design a teahouse in the context of the cultural exchange between Germany and Japan, and (specifically) as an event for the "Katachi" exhibition which showcased Japanese design and craft in the summer of 2007. Two principal conditions were stipulated for this commission: it had to be built on a small hill next to the museum and the design needed to minimize the risk of vandalism. Kengo Kuma decided to realize the teahouse in the form of a membrane structure that could be easily installed and stored. In his mind's eye, he envisioned a soft and light architecture. Kuma also campaigned for the preservation of the mature trees at the hill. While the top of the small hill is completely bare, its base is surrounded by six trees, each rising to height of 25 meters. Since the teahouse would be relatively small, it would be erected without difficulty and the presence of the trees would not create a conflict. The challenge lay in how to translate the idea of a teahouse as a membrane structure that can be disassembled and stored into reality. Our chief considerations were with regard to the type of membrane construction, the membrane material and the costs.

Das Teehaus sieht aus wie eine Erdnussschale, Golfbälle oder eine Figur aus einem Anime-Film. Für einen Freund, dem ich es auf einem Foto zeigte, sah es aus wie eine große Raupe. In seinem Inneren empfindet man eine schwebend-leichte Weite und ein eigenartiges Gefühl der Schwerelosigkeit, und man kann den Sonnenstand und die Veränderungen ihrer Helligkeit wahrnehmen. Bei Dunkelheit gleicht das Teehaus einem überdimensionalen Lichtkörper.

Kengo Kuma erhielt den Auftrag zum Entwurf eines Teehauses im Rahmen des deutsch-japanischen Kulturaustauschs, als ein Event zur Ausstellung „Katachi", die im Sommer 2007 Design und Handwerk aus Japan präsentierte. An diesen Auftrag waren im Großen und Ganzen zwei Bedingungen geknüpft: Das Teehaus sollte auf einem kleinen Hügel neben dem Museum stehen, und das Risiko mutwilliger Beschädigung war zu berücksichtigen. Kengo Kuma dachte sich ein Teehaus mit einer Membrankonstruktion aus, das einfach aufzubauen und aufzubewahren wäre. Nach seiner Vorstellung sollte es ein luftig leichtes, weiches Bauwerk werden. Er plädierte auch dafür, die großen Bäume an dem Hügel stehen zu lassen. Die Kuppe des kleinen Hügels ist ganz frei, um den Hügel herum stehen aber sechs Bäume mit etwa 25 m Höhe. Da das Teehaus relativ klein war, ließ es sich einfach errichten, ohne mit den Bäumen in Konflikt zu geraten. Das Problem war, wie sich ein Teehaus mit einer abbau- und lagerfähigen Membrankonstruktion verwirklichen ließe. Unsere Überlegungen drehten sich vor allem um die Art der Membrankonstruktion, das Membranmaterial und die Kosten.

The tea ceremony is a locus of communication between tea master and guests, it is a form of exchange where body and mind encounter one another stripped bare, for social status or age do not play a role here. Superfluity in any form is banished; simplicity rules. This is also true for the area of the teahouse that subtly suggests soberness and simplicity much rather than luxurious, decorative beauty. "The tearoom is insignificant in appearance. It is smaller than the smallest Japanese house, and its building materials are chosen to create an impression of cultivated poverty. Yet we must remember that all of this is the result of profound artistic contemplation and that all minute details have been chosen with a level of care that is as great as that employed for the most sumptuous of palaces and temples. A good tearoom costs more than a common residential house because the selection of the building material as well as the work performed with the material require extraordinary care and precision."[1] Naturally, the carpenters must be very skilled. The delicacy and fragility of the traditional natural materials such as straw, bamboo and wood, which decay over time and return to nature, express the beauty of all that is transitory. During the tea ceremony, the guests are immersed in the flux of time defined by transitoriness [Unbeständigkeit].
Life becomes palpable in the transience of beauty and a more intimate communication is possible through the shared experience of this atmosphere.

Originally, the plan envisioned a tearoom with a floor area of six *tatami* and a preparation (*mizuya*)[2] of three *tatami*; that is a total floor area of nine *tatami*.[3]

At first, we envisioned two access paths: one from the museum restaurant and another from the path that runs through the park. However, when one takes a look at the position of the teahouse from the perspective of the park, a direct link to the restaurant presents itself as a solution and for this reason a decision was made in favor of a paved path from the restaurant patio. Position and ground plan of the teahouse were then arranged in manner that the tearoom would face east and the preparation room west.

Studies on the shape of the membrane were undertaken in conjunction with the deliberations pertaining to the ground plan. To begin with, we envisioned a membrane structure in the shape of a single dome. However, since there was no imperative correspondence between the spatial structure and the shape of the membrane itself, it was quite a challenge to determine the optimal form. It was at this stage that we had the idea of differentiating between tearoom and preparation room by creating two separate volumes and arranging the whole in such a manner that these two spaces would be connected. Since this effectively determined the respective floor areas and room heights, the entire structure of the building could now be calculated. The configuration of the entrance is vital in the case of an inflatable membrane structure. Since the stability of the entire envelope in a single-layer membrane structure is maintained through the difference between interior and exterior pressure, the entrance must be made airtight. However, since there are no differences between interior and exterior pressure when a double-layer

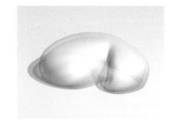

Study model No. 6, Sept. 2005

---

[1] Okakura Kakuzō: The Book of Tea, Mineola, NY 1964, pp. 36.
[2] *mizuya* — lit. "water room" is the word used to describe the preparation room of the teahouse.
[3] The total floor area, comprising the large rectangle measuring nine *tatami* and the rounded bottom edges of the membrane, is roughly 23 m^2.

Study model No. 9, Febr. 2006

Die Teezeremonie ist eine Stätte der Kommunikation zwischen dem Gastgeber und den Gästen. Es ist eine Form des Austauschs, bei dem Körper und Geist sich in einem „nackten" Zustand begegnen, denn Rang und Seniorität spielen hier keine Rolle. Alles Überflüssige wird weggelassen, Einfachheit dominiert. Das gilt ebenso für den Bereich des Teehauses, in dem statt prunkvoller, dekorativer Schönheit in subtiler Weise Mangel und Einfachheit angedeutet werden. „Der Teeraum sieht unscheinbar aus. Er ist kleiner als das kleinste japanische Haus, und seine Baustoffe sind gewählt, den Eindruck kultivierter Armut zu erwecken. Doch müssen wir daran denken, dass dies alles das Ergebnis tiefer künstlerischer Überlegung ist und dass alle Kleinigkeiten mit einer Sorgfalt ausgewählt worden sind, wie sie beim Bau der reichsten Paläste und Tempel nicht größer sein kann. Ein guter Teeraum kostet mehr als ein gewöhnliches Wohnhaus, denn die Auswahl des Baustoffes ebenso wie seine Bearbeitung erfordern außerordentliche Sorgfalt und Genauigkeit."[1] Natürlich müssen die Zimmerleute über besonderes Geschick verfügen. Die Feinheit und die Fragilität der verwendeten natürlichen Materialien wie Stroh, Bambus und Holz, die mit der Zeit zerfallen und zur Natur zurückkehren, bringen die Schönheit des Vergänglichen zum Ausdruck. Bei der Teezeremonie tauchen die Gäste ein in den von Unbeständigkeit geprägten Strom der Zeit. In der Schönheit des Vergänglichen wird das Leben spürbar, und in der gemeinsamen Erfahrung dieser Atmosphäre wird eine umso intimere Kommunikation möglich.

Bei den anfänglichen Planungen gingen wir aus von einem Teeraum von sechs *tatami* und einem Anrichteraum (*mizuya*[2]) von drei *tatami*, zusammen also neun *tatami* Grundfläche[3]. Zunächst hatten wir zwei Zugangswege vorgesehen: einen vom Museumsrestaurant her und einen vom Parkweg her. Betrachtet man jedoch die Position des Teehauses vom Park her, so kommt eine direkte Verbindung zum Restaurant in Betracht, und deshalb haben wir uns für einen mit Steinplatten ausgelegten Zugang von der Gartenterrasse des Restaurants her entschieden. Position und Grundriss des Teehauses wurden dann so angeordnet, dass der Teeraum nach Osten und der Anrichteraum nach Westen ausgerichtet ist.

Passend zum Grundriss haben wir gleichzeitig Überlegungen zur Form der Membrankonstruktion angestellt. Anfangs war eine Membrankonstruktion in Form einer einzigen Kuppel vorgesehen. Da aber keine zwingende Verbindung zwischen der Raumstruktur und der Form der Membrankonstruktion bestand, war es nicht so einfach, die optimale Form zu bestimmen. An diesem Punkt kam uns die Idee, Teeraum und Anrichteraum in zwei gesonderte räumliche Formen zu differenzieren und das Ganze so anzuordnen, dass die beiden Raumkörper verbunden sind. Da dadurch die jeweiligen Flächen und Raumhöhen vorgegeben waren, ließ sich nun die Struktur des ganzen Bauwerks berechnen. Bei einer pneumatischen Membrankonstruktion kommt es darauf an, wie der Zugang gestaltet wird. Da bei Konstruktionen mit einer einzigen Membran die ganze Hülle durch den Unterschied zwischen Innendruck und Außendruck stabil gehalten wird, muss der Zugang luftdicht verschlossen sein. Weil es aber bei Konstruktionen mit Doppelmembranen keine Druckunterschiede zwischen innen und außen gibt, hat man Freiheit bei

[1] Okakura Kakuzō: Das Buch vom Tee. Wiesbaden 1954, S. 36f.
[2] Mit *mizuya* – wörtlich: „Wasserraum" – bezeichnet man den Vorbereitungsbereich des Teehauses.
[3] Zusammen mit den freien Flächen zwischen dem großen Rechteck der gesamten 9-*tatami*-Fläche und den kreisrunden unteren Rändern der Hülle ergibt sich eine Gesamtgrundfläche von etwa 23 m².

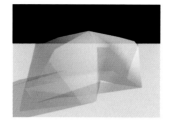

Study model No. 10, Febr. 2006

membrane structure is used, one has greater freedom in the design of the entrance. Naturally, the costs for a structure with two membranes are higher. Moreover, if one takes the preparatory steps — essential to the tea ceremony and undertaken in the preparation room — into account, a single-membrane structure with an airtight entrance (e.g. with air locks) is impractical since it restricts movement quite considerably. Overcoming such restrictions would require additional building components and increase costs. For these reasons, we decided to proceed with a double-membrane inflatable structure.

In its final form, the outer membrane of the teahouse has a diameter of 4.6 m and the outer membrane of the preparation room one of 4.15 m; the corresponding dimensions for the inner membrane are 3.8 m and 3.25 m diameter, respectively. The total length is 8.37 m. Stability for the spherical form of the inflatable membrane structure is provided by changing the inner and outer radius.

The two membranes are connected via some 400 strap links; the distance between the two membranes fluctuates between 40 cm at the base and 100 cm at the apex of the larger "balloon." Two possible connection methods were discussed during the design stage: in one, the membranes are stitched together like stacked tori; in the other, which was ultimately chosen, the membranes are connected via cables or straps. Since the first method is realized by geometrically dividing the sphere, heterogeneous radiations will result. The strap links are stretched when the structure is inflated. While the membrane is being inflated, it is evident that air in fact creates the structure. This geometrical sphere is theoretically possible and computable, but it is difficult to realize because each individual strap link has a different length and each section of fabric a different size. The entire double membrane was manufactured by the Italian firm Canobbio S.p.A; it is only thanks to the high technical standards of this specialized firm that this project could be realized.

Selecting the appropriate material proved just as difficult because the material places limits on the structural methods and shapes that could be used. At first, we considered using a natural fabric to create the air membrane structure. We were inspired to contemplate this option by a vision of an airy-soft tearoom constructed of a white, translucent material reminiscent of *shōji* or *washi*.[4] It appears, however, that no natural material exists which can be used for such an exterior membrane structure. The client had moreover requested a highly flame resistant material. We considered using kenaf[5] as possibly being suitable for the membrane material, but it has a slight brownish cast and is not translucent. Had it been possible to render it translucent by some means, an application may have been considered. However, it became clear that this is barely feasible with the currently available technology. The next material that we looked at was ETFE[6], which is highly transparent. We considered using the transparency and applying Japanese paper (*washi*) on the inside. The problem we encountered here was less the application with adhesives than the hardness of ETFE, which renders application in a form with pronounced curvatures very difficult and would also not have been suitable for folds. All this did not

---

[4] *Shōji* are paper sliding doors; *washi* is a traditional Japanese paper made of plant fibers.

[5] Kenaf (hibiscus cannabinus): a tropical annual, a species of hibiscus, from which (textile) fiber and oil are obtained.

[6] ETFE (ethylene tetrafluoroethylene) is a lightweight, highly translucent polymer plastic. In architecture, ETFE foils are primarily used for membrane structures.

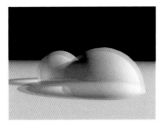

Study model No. 17, Oct. 2006

der Gestaltung des Zugangs. Ein Bauwerk aus zwei Hüllen verursacht natürlich höhere Kosten. Berücksichtigt man ferner die für die Teezeremonie notwendigen Vorbereitungen im Anrichteraum, ist der luftdichte Zugang (z.B. mit einer Schleuse) bei einer Ein-Membran-Konstruktion unpraktisch, da er die Bewegungsfreiheit ziemlich einschränkt. Um solche Einschränkungen zu umgehen, bräuchte man wiederum zusätzliche Bauteile, was die Kosten erhöhen würde. So haben wir uns letztlich für eine pneumatische Konstruktion mit Doppelmembran entschieden. In seiner endgültigen Form hat die äußere Hülle des Teehauses einen Durchmesser von 4,60 m und die des Anrichteraums einen von 4,15 m, die innere Hülle jeweils 3,80 m beziehungsweise 3,25 m Durchmesser; die Gesamtlänge beträgt 8,37 m. Die geometrische Kugelform der pneumatischen Membrankonstruktion erhält durch Veränderung des inneren und des äußeren Radius Stabilität.
Die beiden Hüllen werden von etwa 400 Verbindungsbändern verbunden/zusammengehalten; der Abstand zwischen den beiden Hüllen schwankt zwischen 40 cm an der Basis und 100 cm am höchsten Punkt des größeren „Ballons". Bei der Planung standen zwei Verbindungstechniken zur Diskussion: Bei der einen werden die Hüllen wie übereinandergestapelte Wülste vernäht; bei der schließlich angewandten Technik werden die beiden Hüllen durch Bänder verbunden. Da man bei der ersten Technik den Kugelkörper geometrisch aufteilt, entstehen heterogene Strahlungen. Die Verbindungsbänder werden in der aufgeblasenen Form gespannt. Beim Aufblasen der Hülle kann man gut erkennen, dass die Luft den Baukörper bildet. Diese geometrische Kugelform ist theoretisch möglich und berechenbar, in

Wirklichkeit aber nur schwer zu realisieren, denn jedes einzelne Verbindungsband hat eine andere Länge und jede der etwa 80 Stoffbahnen hat eine andere Größe. Die gesamte Doppelhülle haben wir von der italienischen Firma Canobbio S.p.A. konfektionieren lassen; nur dank des hohen technischen Standards dieser Spezialfirma konnte das Projekt überhaupt verwirklicht werden.

Die Wahl des richtigen Materials erwies sich ebenfalls als schwierig. Denn durch das Material werden die möglichen Konstruktionsmethoden und Formen begrenzt. Zunächst haben wir daran gedacht, die pneumatische Membrankonstruktion in natürlichem Gewebematerial auszuführen. Dabei leitete uns die Vorstellung eines luftig-leichten Teeraums aus einem weißen, durchscheinenden Material, das an shōji oder washi[4] erinnern sollte. Anscheinend gibt es aber kein natürliches Material, das sich für eine solche Freiluftkonstruktion verwenden lässt. Außerdem hatten die Auftraggeber ein schwer entflammbares Material verlangt. Zunächst waren wir noch davon ausgegangen, dass Kenaf[5] sich als Membranmaterial eignen könnte. Aber Kenaf-Gewebe ist leicht bräunlich gefärbt und nicht durchscheinend. Falls es sich irgendwie durchscheinend machen ließe, wäre eine Verwendung eventuell in Frage gekommen. Es stellte sich aber heraus, dass dies mit der derzeitigen Technologie kaum zu machen ist.
Als Nächstes kam ETFE[6] in Frage. Da ETFE eine gute Transluzenz besitzt, wollten wir diese Eigenschaft nutzen und die Innenseite mit washi bekleben. Das Problem dabei aber war weniger das Bekleben, sondern die Härte der ETFE-Folien, deren Verwendung bei einer Form mit so hohem Krümmungsgrad

[4] Shōji sind Papierschiebetüren; washi ist traditionelles japanisches Papier aus Pflanzenfasern.
[5] Kenaf (Hibiscus cannabinus): eine einjährige tropische Pflanze aus der Familie der Malvengewächse, aus der (Textil-)Fasern und Öl gewonnen werden.
[6] ETFE (Ethylen-Tetrafluorethylen) ist ein Kunststoffmaterial mit geringem Gewicht und hoher Lichtdurchlässigkeit. Einsatz finden ETFE-Folien in der Architektur vor allem bei Membrankonstruktionen.

satisfy our desire to create a structure with a soft appearance. In the end we settled on using Tenara.[7] Although not a natural material, it is soft, white and light and thus corresponded with our ideas. When we actually touched the material, it felt very soft and fine and we were able to imagine that we could create the impression of white *shōji* paper with this translucent white material.

We also wanted to utilize the characteristics and white color of this material to enhance the lighting of the teahouse. The membrane was to function as a kind of lamp shade and create an evenly distributed light in the interior. LED lights, fitted in the connection between the membrane and the foundation, were considered for lighting despite the maintenance requirements. Once the membrane is fastened, the source of light was to remain hidden. The LED lights were manufactured in Japan and donated by the firm Matsushita.[8]

One of the most challenging aspects of this project was the storage of the membrane structure. In the beginning we considered opening up the floor with a horizontal sliding shutter that would be easy to open. The membrane, stored underneath, would then be inflated and raised. The problems presented by this solution were that the horizontal shutter would have to be entirely waterproof and that the storage chamber would have to comply with certain conditions to preserve the membrane in good condition. The membrane should be stored in dry conditions throughout the year. Dampness may lead to mold, resulting in a soiled appearance or unpleasant odor. In the end, we decided to use a portable membrane structure and

blower to be stored in the museum. The membrane and blower are simply transported to the outside location when needed and the membrane is attached to the foundation for set up. This eliminates the cost of the shutter, the subterranean storage space and maintenance efforts. Making the membrane structure fully portable means that it can be inflated wherever a power outlet exists, indoors or outdoors, thus considerably expanding the uses to which the teahouse can be put.

Next, we were faced with the task of determining how the membrane structure would be attached to the foundation. A simple solution was called for to ensure that the membrane structure could be set up without much ado; wind resistance and waterproof connections were additional essential considerations. Kuma suggested that zippers be used. A zipper would secure the membrane to the foundation and be easy for anyone to set up. The set up of the teahouse begins with attaching all zippers along the sides to the aluminum channel that is integrated into the foundation. Then two zippers on the inside and outside of the membrane are zipped up from the inside. A zipper cover ensures that the structure is waterproof. The blower is also portable, like the membrane structure. Making it portable expands the range of locations in which the teahouse can be used, and also obviates the need for a separate storage space for the blower. When the teahouse is set up on the hill, as shown here, the blower is placed at a certain distance to minimize noise from the blower. An appropriate power source has been provided for this purpose; an in-ground blower pipe and an exposed hose lead to

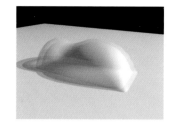

Study model No. 19, Dec. 2006

[7] Tenara is a synthetic material made from ePTFE (expanded polytetrafluoroethylene); highly versatile for use in architecture. GORE® TENARA™ Architectural Fabric, 3T40HFG manufactured by the American firm E. L. Gore & Associates, was used for the teahouse.
[8] Detailed company information: Matsushita Electrical Works, Ltd.; Panasonic Electrical Works, Ltd.; Vossloh-Schwabe GmbH, Lüdenscheid

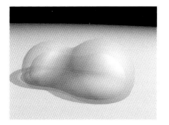

Study model No. 25, Jan 2007

schwierig wäre und selbst in gefalteter Form kaum in Frage käme. Deshalb überlegten wir, ob sich ETFE nicht verwenden ließe, indem wir statt einer gekrümmten Gesamtfläche die Fläche aufteilten und die einzelnen Teile auf Rahmen befestigten. Doch dies entsprach nicht unserer Idee von weicher Architektur. So entschieden wir uns letzten Endes für Tenara[7]. Das ist zwar auch kein natürliches Material, aber da es weich, weiß und leicht ist, entsprach es unseren Vorstellungen. Als wir dann das wirkliche Material abtasteten, fühlte es sich sehr weich und fein an, und wir konnten uns vorstellen, dass sich mit diesem durchscheinend-weißen Gewebe der Eindruck des weißen *shōji*-Papiers erreichen ließe.

Eigenschaften und weiße Farbe des Materials wollten wir auch nutzen, wenn das ganze Teehaus mit Beleuchtung ausgestattet würde. Die Hülle sollte eine Art Lampenschirm bilden und gleichmäßig leuchten. Als Lichtquelle kamen unter Berücksichtigung des Wartungsaufwands LED-Leuchten in Frage, die unterhalb der Membran im Basisrahmen untergebracht wurden. Wenn die Membran einmal befestigt war, sollte man nicht erkennen, woher das Licht kommt. Die Leuchtkörper sind ein japanisches Fabrikat, das von der Firma Matsushita[8] gestiftet wurde.

Ein kniffliges schwieriges Problem bei diesem Projekt war die Aufbewahrung der Membrankonstruktion. Anfangs hatten wir dafür einen unterirdischen Lagerraum mit einem horizontalen Ziehportal vorgesehen, das sich einfach öffnen ließe. Die zuvor darin verstaute Membran würde dann mit Luft aufgepumpt und vollständig aufgerichtet. Probleme waren dabei die notwendige absolute Wasserun-

durchlässigkeit des horizontalen Portals und die Bedingungen im Aufbewahrungsraum der Membran. Für die Konservierung des Membranmaterials wäre ganzjährig trockenes Wetter ideal. Feuchtigkeit würde dagegen allmählich zu unerwünschter Schimmelbildung, Verschmutzung oder Geruchsbildung führen. Schließlich kamen wir auf die Idee, die Teile der Membrankonstruktion und das Gebläse transportabel zu machen und diese für gewöhnlich im Museumsgebäude zu deponieren. Bei dieser Lösung würden Membran und Gebläse nur dann nach außen transportiert, wenn es aus bestimmtem Anlass erforderlich wäre, und die Membran dann einfach an der Basis befestigt. Außerdem könnte man so die Kosten für das Portal, den unterirdischen Lagerraum und ihre Instandhaltung einsparen. Bei einer transportablen Konstruktion ist es möglich, sie überall aufzupumpen, wo es eine Stromquelle gibt, und damit würden sich die Nutzungsmöglichkeiten dieses Teehauses wesentlich erweitern.

Anschließend beschäftigten wir uns mit der Frage, wie die Membrankonstruktion an der Basis befestigt werden sollte. Anzustreben war eine einfache Lösung, damit man die Membrankonstruktion ohne besondere Umstände aufbauen könnte. Es müsste auch dafür gesorgt werden, dass alles wind- und wasserfest ist. Kengo Kuma schlug vor, Reißverschlüsse zu benutzen. Damit kann wirklich jeder umgehen und die Hülle befestigen. Bei der konkreten Ausführung werden zuerst alle Reißverschluss-Seitenteile an der an der Basis angebrachten Aluminiumschiene befestigt. Anschließend werden die beiden Reißverschlüsse auf der Innenseite und der Außenseite der Membranhülle von der Innenseite her geschlossen.

---

[7] Tenara ist ein in der Architektur vielseitig verwendbares Gewebe aus dem Kunststoff ePTFE (expandiertes PolyTetraFluorEthylen) Für das Teehaus wurde GORE® TENARA™ Architectural Fabric, 3T40HFG von der US-amerikanischen Firma W. L. Gore & Associates benutzt.
[8] Genaue Firmenangaben: Matsushita Electrical Works, Ltd.; Panasonic Electrical Works, Ltd.; Vossloh-Schwabe GmbH, Lüdenscheid.

the membrane. The blower was manufactured by Gustav Nolting GmbH of Germany and generates a constant pressure of 1,500 (±30) Pascal.

This project was realized on the basis of plans created by the Japanese architect Kengo Kuma and the outstanding technology provided by the German structural engineer Gerd Schmid (formTL GmbH).[9] And it now resides in the country that can be justly called the home of membrane structures, which were developed by Frei Otto. As a symbol of the cultural exchange between Japan and Germany, the teahouse plays a not insignificant role in the age of globalization.

This inflatable membrane structure, which rises effortlessly and lightly when needed and which has been likened to a white blossom by the museum's director, Ulrich Schneider, has an air of transience. It was clearly fitting that this teahouse should be constructed not of a solid material (as a safeguard against vandalism) but from a weak and soft material.

This might lead one to ask whether the use of weak materials and inflatable architecture are specifically Japanese in nature. In contrast to German buildings, chiefly made of stone, wood is the principal material used in Japan. Seeking to interpret the meaning of this teahouse solely on the basis of this contrast would be too facile an approach, however. For, prior to the advent of stone architecture, Germany too was home to many timber-built structures and modern membrane structures are a technology that was first developed in Germany.

On the occasion of the inauguration of the teahouse, a guest remarked that the structure had very little of the Japanese about it. If one were to compare our teahouse to classic examples like *Tai'an* and *Jo'an*[10], one might well agree because it is entirely novel both in form and in material. To anyone, however, who recognizes it as a site where the Way of the Tea is cultivated, this teahouse is without a doubt Japanese.

What is the first thought that springs to mind upon seeing this structure: that it is probably Japanese or that it is a teahouse? Regardless of the answer, even if a misunderstanding were to occur, what matters is that this structure offers an opportunity to understand Japan and Germany. To my mind, this would be a true exchange and form of communication, from which new beginnings can develop. We would be honored if you could encounter something of both Japan and Germany — without worrying about misunderstandings — in our teahouse.

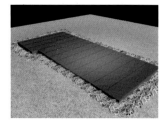

Horizontal shutter, closed position
Horizontaler Verschluss in
geschlossenem Zustand

[9] formTL, a German engineering firm, played an essential role in the realization of this structure.
[10] *Tai'an* and *Jo'an*: two "exemplary" classic teahouses by Sen no Rikyū (1582) and Oda Yūrakusai (1618).

Horizontal shutter, opened position
Horizontaler Verschluss in
geöffnetem Zustand

Wasserdichtigkeit wird dadurch erreicht, dass die oben am Reißverschluss angebrachte Abdeckung den Verschlussteil verbirgt.

Auch das Gebläse lässt sich zusammen mit der Membrankonstruktion transportieren. Das macht das Teehaus vielseitig einsetzbar; außerdem erübrigt sich so ein Abstellraum für das Gebläse. Wenn das Teehaus wie dieses Mal auf seinem Platz auf dem Hügel steht, haben wir dafür gesorgt, dass das Gebläse in einem gewissen Abstand aufgestellt wird, um Störungen durch das Motorengeräusch zu vermeiden. An den Standort wurde eine passende Stromquelle gelegt; von dort bis zur Basis der Membranhülle führen eine unterirdische Röhre und ein freiverlegter Schlauch. Unser Gebläse ist ein Gerät der deutschen Firma Nolting, das einen konstanten Druck von 1500 (±30) Pascal erzeugt.

Unser Projekt wurde nach den Plänen von Kengo Kuma, einem japanischen Architekten, mit Hilfe der hervorragenden Technik des deutschen Ingenieurs Gerd Schmid (Firma form TL)[9] verwirklicht, in dem Land, das man als Heimat der von Frei Otto entwickelten Membrankonstruktion bezeichnen darf. Als Symbol des deutsch-japanischen Kulturaustauschs kommt ihm im Zeitalter der Globalisierung besondere Bedeutung zu. Dieses als pneumatische Membrankonstruktion bezeichnete Bauwerk, das sich bei gegebenem Anlass schwebend leicht erhebt und von Ulrich Schneider, dem Direktor des Museums, mit einer weißen Blüte verglichen wurde, hat etwas Vergängliches an sich. Deshalb war es für dieses Teehaus wohl passend, es nicht aus festem Material (zum Schutz gegen Vandalismus), sondern aus schwachem und weichem Material zu bauen. Hier könnte man sich fragen, ob die Verwendung von schwachem Material und pneumatische Architektur denn spezifisch japanisch sind. Im Gegensatz zu Bauten in Deutschland, die in der großen Mehrzahl aus Stein gebaut sind, wird in Japan überwiegend mit Holz gearbeitet. Doch ein Verständnis dieses Teehauses, das von diesem Gegensatz ausgeht, wäre zu einfach, denn vor der Steinarchitektur wurde in Deutschland sowohl in Stein als auch in Holz gebaut, und moderne Membrankonstruktionen sind ursprünglich eine in Deutschland entwickelte Technologie.

Bei der Eröffnung des Teehauses hat einer der Anwesenden geäußert, dass dieses Bauwerk so gar nichts Japanisches an sich habe. Vergleicht man unser Teehaus mit klassischen Beispielen wie *Tai'an* und *Jo'an*[10], so ist es wohl kaum als japanisch zu bezeichnen, denn auch seine Form und die Baustoffe sind völlig neuartig. Doch für den, der darin eine Stätte zur Kultivierung des Teewegs zu erkennen vermag, dürfte dieses Teehaus gewiss als japanisch gelten. Was kommt Ihnen bei der Begegnung mit dieser Konstruktion zuerst in den Sinn? Dass sie wahrscheinlich japanisch ist oder dass es sich um ein Teehaus handelt? Auch wenn es vielleicht ein Missverständnis sein mag, wichtig ist auf jeden Fall, in diesem Bauwerk Japan und Deutschland zu entdecken und zu verstehen. Dies wäre für mich ein wirklicher Austausch und eine Form der Kommunikation, aus der sich Neues entwickeln kann. Wir würden uns glücklich schätzen, wenn Sie — ohne Scheu vor Missverständnissen — in unserem Teehaus Japan und Deutschland wiederfinden könnten.

---

[9] form TL, eine deutsches Ingenieurbüro, war maßgeblich an der Realisierung des Bauwerks beteiligt.
[10] *Tai'an* und *Jo'an*: zwei „mustergültige" klassische Teehäuser von Sen no Rikyū (1582) und Oda Yūrakusai (1618).

Katinka Temme / Maria-Isabel Martín-Peláez

Collaboration in Architecture

Architektur als Zusammenarbeit

Test installation of membrane by museum staff and installation team from Canobbio S.p.A., Italy

Testaufbau der Membrane durch Museumsmitarbeiter und Monteure des italienischen Unternehmens Canobbio S.p.A.

The first part of this article was written by Katinka Temme from Kengo Kuma & Associates, and the second by Maria-Isabel Martín-Peláez from the Building Department of the City of Frankfurt. Both texts express the fact that the two parties' collaboration was the only practicable way to realise the teahouse.

With an increasing number of international projects, Kengo Kuma & Associates are facing the challenge of how to construct buildings abroad that are inspired by and react to the local context, while continuing to represent the office's philosophy and buildings in Japan.

In Japan, architects collaborate closely with engineers, general contractors, craftspeople and manufacturers developing appropriate and sometimes outstanding details of the design. Compared to American or European practice, the architects draw only a few, fundamental details. Specific details are often developed in collaboration between crafts-people and designers at the construction site. The hierarchy is flatter than in Europe and work is based on mutual respect and trust, with the architectural idea as both the starting point and the goal.

For the teahouse project, the team was initially made up of the Museum (the client), represented by its director Ulrich Schneider; free curator Ms Miki Shimokawa; the City of Frankfurt, represented by Peter Maurer and Maria-I. Martín-Peláez; the structural engineer Gerd Schmidt from formTL; the general contractor and sponsor Takenaka Europe, represented by Mr Iwasa and Mr Randau; the membrane manufacturer Taiyo Europe

Dieser Beitrag besteht aus einem ersten Teil, den Katinka Temme von Kengo Kuma & Associates verfasst hat, und einem zweiten Teil, den Maria-I. Martín-Peláez für das Hochbauamt der Stadt Frankfurt am Main beigesteuert hat. In beiden Texten kommt zum Ausdruck, dass die Zusammenarbeit beider Parteien der einzig gangbare Weg zur Realisierung des Teehauses war.

Mit wachsender Anzahl internationaler Projekte stellt sich für Kengo Kuma & Associates die Aufgabe, wie Gebäude im Ausland zu realisieren sind, die zwar durch den lokalen Kontext inspiriert sind und auf diesen zurückwirken, gleichzeitig aber auch die Philosophie des Büros und seiner Bauten in Japan repräsentieren und fortführen sollen. Architekten arbeiten in Japan eng mit Ingenieuren und Generalunternehmern, mit Handwerkern und Herstellern zusammen, um geeignete und teilweise auch herausragende Details einer Architektur zu erarbeiten. Verglichen mit US-amerikanischen oder europäischen Standards zeichnen Architekten daher eher wenige und nur fundamentale Details. Spezifische Details werden oft erst auf der Baustelle in Zusammenarbeit zwischen Handwerkern und Planern gelöst. Anders als in Europa basiert die Zusammenarbeit auf einer eher flachen Hierarchie und auf gegenseitigem Respekt, wobei die architektonische Idee stets Start- wie auch Zielpunkt ist.
Beim Teehaus-Projekt bestand das Team zu Beginn aus dem Museum als Bauherr mit seinem Direktor Ulrich Schneider und der freien Kuratorin Miki Shimokawa, den Ingenieuren Peter Maurer und Maria Martín-Peláez als Vertreter der Stadt Frankfurt, dem Bauingenieur Gerd Schmid von formTL, dem

(which later left the team), represented by Mr Matsumoto and Mr Kleibel; and Kengo Kuma & Associates, represented by Kengo Kuma, Takumi Saikawa and myself, Katinka Temme. In the collaboration we discussed financial, legal and logistic parameters at length, but not aesthetic or constructional details. For our office, this was an astonishing new experience.

The Museum's idea was to bypass the sparse state funds and find sponsors to donate the teahouse to the Museum für Angewandte Kunst Frankfurt. Over the course of the collaboration, we were distressed to discover that it is not that easy to give presents to German institutions. Having found several willing and enthusiastic sponsors in Japan, we had to figure out the details of the international collaboration. Demarcation is always a delicate undertaking. In Europe and the USA, a working partnership is practically based on a contract and a fee agreement. In Japan, however, legally binding documents are not as essential as mutual trust and the promise of future collaboration. This way of thinking is very supportive for the creative process, as it allows work to proceed quickly, and engenders a valuable, almost intimate relationship between designer and producer.

In addition to the discussions on demarcation, the team had to face several statutory provisions and local conditions that greatly affected the design and the schedule. People's scepticism focused on how to protect a light and elegantly "soft" building from vandalism; this discussion even culminated in the shocking proposal to cover the teahouse in a secondary steel skin. Different concepts of lightness became evi-

dent, as did the different ways of having discussions: while the Japanese tended to be relaxed and probably underestimated the situation, the Germans put forward worst-case scenarios.

After a series of meetings, the team decided to make the teahouse removable and inflatable. While this seemed a great idea on a conceptual level, the issue of how to realise it resulted in a lengthy planning and design process, with almost monthly meetings in Frankfurt and almost daily e-mails, telephone conferences and fax correspondences. Several dates for the opening were announced and then postponed because of the need to solve new challenges. Nevertheless, this process was certainly very necessary — and ultimately beneficial — for both the project and the team, although it initially demanded a great deal of effort, nerves and stamina.

The primary objective, for Kengo Kuma & Associates, was to translate the idea of the traditional teahouse into contemporary and unique architecture, and thus strengthen the friendly exchange between Japan and Germany. The Museum and the City, although grateful for the gift, were worried about future maintenance and costs. The structural engineer was nervous about the many revisions of the complicated drawings, and was a great support to KKAA in devising a new structural solution, as well as allaying some of the client's anxieties.

Once the final design was decided and additional sponsorship found, the collaboration went very well. The structural engineer, formTL, produced the final execution drawings in a

Assembling the LED channel
Die LED-Rinne wird bestückt

Testing the LED channel
Test der LED-Rinne

Generalunternehmer und Sponsor Takenaka Europe, vertreten durch die Herrn Iwasa und Randau, dem später abgesprungenen Membran-Hersteller Taiyo Europe mit den Herren Matsumoto und Kleibel und Kengo Kuma & Associates, vertreten durch die Herren Kuma, Saikawa, und Katinka Temme, der Verfasserin dieser Zeilen. Bei der Zusammenarbeit wurden ausführlich finanzielle, juristische und logistische Vorgaben diskutiert, nicht jedoch ästhetische oder konstruktive Sachverhalte. Dies war für unser Büro eine überraschend neue Erfahrung.

Die Idee des Museums war, die spärlichen staatlichen Quellen zu umgehen und Sponsoren zu finden, die das Teehaus als Geschenk an das Museum für Angewandte Kunst Frankfurt stiften. Im Lauf der Zusammenarbeit stellten wir bekümmert fest, dass es nicht so einfach ist, wie man vermuten würde, deutschen Institutionen etwas zu schenken. Als wir etliche bereitwillige und enthusiastische Sponsoren in Japan gefunden hatten, mussten die Details der Zusammenarbeit des internationalen Teams geklärt werden.

Zuständigkeitsbereiche aufzuteilen ist immer ein sehr heikles Unterfangen. Eine funktionierende Partnerschaft basiert in Europa und den USA pragmatisch auf einem Vertrag und einem Honorarabkommen. In Japan jedoch ist ein bindendes Papier nicht so wichtig wie das gemeinschaftliche Vertrauen mit der Aussicht auf weitere zukünftige Zusammenarbeit. Diese Denkart ist für den kreativen Prozess sehr hilfreich, da sie ein schnelles Vorgehen und eine wertvolle, fast intime Beziehung zwischen Designer und Hersteller erlaubt.

Neben der Diskussion um die Zuständigkeitsbereiche musste sich das Team einigen juristischen Vorgaben und lokalen Bedingungen stellen, die großen Einfluss auf das Design und den Ablauf hatten. Gegenstand der Skepsis war die Frage, wie man ein leichtes und vornehmes „weiches" Gebäude vor Vandalismus schützen kann (sie gipfelte in dem erschreckenden Vorschlag, das Teehaus in ein Stahlhaus einzupacken). Ein anderes Verständnis von Leichtigkeit wie auch ein unterschiedliches Diskussionsverhalten zeichneten sich ab: Während die japanische Seite eher entspannt war und die Situation vermutlich unterbewertete, wartete die deutsche Seite mit Worst-Case-Szenarien auf.

Nach einer Reihe von Treffen zu diesem Thema entschloss sich das Team, das Teehaus abbaubar und aufblasbar zu machen. Während dies aus konzeptioneller Sicht eine großartige Idee zu sein schien, endete die Frage nach der Realisierung in einem langwierigen Planungs- und Designprozess, mit fast monatlichen Treffen in Frankfurt und beinahe täglichen E-Mails, Telefonkonferenzen und Fax-Korrespondenzen. Verschiedene Termine für die Eröffnung wurden anvisiert und aufgrund der Notwendigkeit, diese neuen Herausforderungen zu lösen, wieder aufgeschoben. Dennoch war dieser Prozess für beide Seiten, das Projekt und das Team, sicherlich notwendig und letztendlich auch förderlich, auch wenn er zunächst sehr viel Kraft, Nerven und Durchhaltevermögen gefordert hat.
Kengo Kuma & Associates' Anliegen war es, die Idee des traditionellen Teehauses in eine zeitgemäße, einzigartige Architektur zu übersetzen und damit den freundschaftlichen

very short period and with a high level of precision, which satisfied both the Germans and the Japanese. Ultimately, the idea of "breathing architecture" that emerged from the numerous passionate discussions bound the individuals together into a big team with a single goal.

During the construction phase, the representatives of the City of Frankfurt were extremely helpful. As both the architect (in Japan) and the structural engineer (at the Lake of Constance) were too far away to be present daily, Ms Martín-Peláez and Mr Maurer became the extremely valuable construction managers. The City was also a good partner, involving local firms in smaller tasks, such as landscaping, mechanical and electrical engineering. Finally, and very much in the Japanese tradition, several details were developed at the site, or through e-mail or telephone feedback from the design team. We received wonderful support for the opening from the tea master Sōshin Kimura (Urasenke) and his team, as well as from the Museum staff.

The key to realising the teahouse was doubtless the collaborative process. Many parameters that determined the concept and the design of "breathing architecture" could not have been predicted from Japan. Furthermore, it was Kengo Kuma & Associates' first building in Germany. Although we already had connections to some German manufacturers and consultants, we had to rely on the local team to make up for our lack of the intensive network we would be used to in Japan. In this special situation, it was very helpful to have Takenaka Corporation as a bridge between the two worlds.

The teahouse project was a valuable experience in building in Europe for Kengo Kuma & Associates, and has since helped us in many further European projects, such as in the UK, Hungary and Switzerland. Each team member showed great enthusiasm, was willing to put in extraordinary effort, and learned from the team — not just a great deal about architecture, but also a little about different cultures (even different cultures within Germany). What had begun eight months before as a loud and adamant German discussion was repeatedly mollified by the Japanese team members, who returned the focus to the construction, and finally culminated in last-minute hectic telephone calls to Italy. But at the end, all that mattered was the pleasure of the smell and taste of a bowl of tea.

Kengo Kuma & Associates would like to thank wholeheartedly all the team members, many of whom became good friends, for their willingness to take on the challenge of this cultural exchange project, and for their support in realising the Teahouse Frankfurt.

Katinka Temme[1]

---

[1] Kengo Kuma & Associates

Filler neck for compressed air
Einfüllstutzen für die Pressluft

Austausch zwischen Japan und Deutschland zu stärken. Das Museum und die Stadt, zwar dankbar für das Geschenk, waren über die zukünftige Erhaltung und die Kosten besorgt. Der Tragwerksplaner war bestürzt über die vielen Änderungen auf den komplizierten Zeichnungen und unterstützte KKAA großartig, indem er nicht nur eine neue Konstruktionslösung fand, sondern auch mithalf, die Ängste der Bauherrenseite zu beheben. Als das endgültige Design beschlossen war und zusätzliche Sponsoren gefunden wurden, lief die Zusammenarbeit sehr gut. Der Tragwerksplaner, formTL, fasste die letzten Ausführungszeichnungen in extrem kurzer Zeit und mit großer Präzision zusammen, was sowohl dem japanischen als auch dem deutschen Gemüt entgegenkam. Letztendlich siegte die aus unzähligen leidenschaftlichen Baubesprechungen hervorgegangene Idee der „breathing architecture" und schweißte die Individuen zu einem großen Team zusammen, das auf ein Ziel konzentriert war. Während der Konstruktionsphase waren die Vertreter der Stadt Frankfurt sehr hilfreich. Da die Architekten (in Japan) und der Bauingenieur (am Bodensee) zu weit entfernt waren, um täglich zur Seite zu stehen, wurden Maria Martín-Peláez und Peter Maurer, als gleichsam verlängerter Arm der Planer, zu einer wertvollen Bauaufsicht. Die Stadt war auch ein guter Partner, um lokale Firmen mit kleineren Aufgaben, wie zum Beispiel der Landschaftsgestaltung, der mechanischen und elektrischen Entwicklung, zu involvieren. Zum Schluss wurden der japanischen Mentalität entsprechend viele Details auf der Baustelle oder mit Hilfe von E-Mails oder Telefongesprächen gelöst. Für die Eröffnung erhielten wir die wunderbare

Unterstützung des Teemeisters Sōshin Kimura (Urasenke) und seines Teams, wie auch der Belegschaft des Museums. Insgesamt war der Schlüssel zur Realisierung des Teehauses sicherlich der gemeinschaftliche Prozess. Viele Vorgaben, die das Konzept und das Design der „atmenden Architektur" beeinflussten, waren von Japan aus unvorhersehbar. Für Kengo Kuma & Associates war es darüber hinaus das erste Gebäude in Deutschland. Obwohl wir bereits einige Kontakte zu deutschen Herstellern und Beratern hatten, mussten wir uns auf das Team vor Ort verlassen, um den Mangel eines intensiven Netzwerks, an das wir aus Japan gewöhnt waren, auszugleichen. In dieser speziellen Situation war es sehr hilfreich, Takenaka Corporation als Brücke zwischen beiden Welten zu haben. Für Kengo Kuma & Associates war das Teehaus-Projekt eine wertvolle Erfahrung in Bezug auf Bauen in Europa, die uns inzwischen bei vielen weiteren europäischen Projekten, etwa in England, Ungarn und der Schweiz, sehr geholfen hat. Jedes Mitglied zeigte viel Enthusiasmus, war zu außergewöhnlichen Anstrengungen bereit und lernte von dem Team nicht nur viel über Architektur, sondern auch ein bisschen über die unterschiedlichen Kulturen (selbst innerhalb Deutschlands). Was acht Monate zuvor als eine laute und hartnäckige deutsche Diskussion begann, immer wieder beschwichtigt durch die japanischen Teammitglieder, die den Fokus zurück auf die Architektur brachten, gipfelte in letzter Minute in hektischen und lebhaften Telefonaten nach Italien. Doch am Schluss zählen einzig der Geruch und der Geschmack einer Tasse Tee. Kengo Kuma & Associates möchte von ganzem Herzen allen Teammitgliedern, von

With a very short construction period of just three months, the Modern Teahouse was planned by Kengo Kuma & Associates and realised by an international team in a highly collaborative and creative team effort. Four different languages were sometimes spoken at the construction site; the site meetings with the Japanese architect were followed by strange trilingual telephone calls to Japan and Italy.

The teahouse membrane was produced in Milan, Italy, and the manufacturer attended the construction site in Frankfurt just minutes before completion. For the prefabrication of the membrane, the engineering office FormTL from Radolfzell in Germany sent a very detailed construction document and shop drawing to Italy. The Japanese construction firm, Takenaka Europe, worked on the building shell, and several smaller local firms provided metalworking, landscaping, and various technical and mechanical installations.

All details were discussed at the site. Changes and further details were then discussed by e-mail or by telephone. The final assembly, shortly before the opening in August, was a team effort between all the participants. At times, 15 people crowded onto the small teahouse platform, while communications buzzed between Tokyo, Frankfurt, Radolfzell and Milan. All participants were filled with enthusiasm and were eager to complete this unique project. The result shows that an idea can be realised successfully despite great distances by collaborative effort and passion.

Maria-Isabel Martín-Peláez[2]

Threading the high performance zipper
Einfädeln des Schwerlastreißverschlusses

---

[2] Building Department of the City of Frankfurt am Main.

In the membrane
In der Membrane

denen viele gute Freunde wurden, für den Willen danken, dieses Wagnis eines kulturellen Austauschs auf sich zu nehmen, und natürlich für die Mitarbeit beim Teehaus Frankfurt.

Katinka Temme[1]

In der sehr kurzen Bauzeit von nur drei Monaten wurde das Modern Teahouse von Kengo Kuma & Associates geplant und von einem internationalen Team von Ausführenden in kooperativer und äußerst kreativer Zusammenarbeit umgesetzt. Auf der Baustelle wurde teilweise viersprachig kommuniziert, auf den Bausitzungen, an denen die japanischen Architekten anwesend waren, kamen zum Teil kuriose mehrsprachige Telefonate nach Japan und parallel nach Italien zustande.
Die Konfektionäre der Teehaus-Membran stammen aus Mailand, Italien. Sie stießen persönlich erst kurz vor Fertigstellung zur Baustelle in Frankfurt. Die Vorfertigung der Membran erfolgte nach detaillierten Plänen und Berechnungen des Ingenieurbüros formTL aus Radolfzell in Italien. Die japanische Konstruktionsfirma Takenaka Europe fertigte den Rohbau, und verschiedene kleinere Unternehmen haben Teilleistungen wie Metallbau, Gartenbau sowie diverse technische Installationsarbeiten erbracht. Alle Details wurden vor Ort besprochen, Änderungen und Detaillierungen per E-Mail oder telefonisch diskutiert und geklärt. Die Endmontage kurz vor der Eröffnung im August erfolgte Hand in Hand zwischen allen Beteiligten. Bis zu 15 Personen befanden sich zugleich auf der kleinen Teehaus-Plattform, wobei gleichzeitig zwischen Tōkyō, Frankfurt, Radolfzell und Mailand kommuniziert wurde. Alle Beteiligten waren mit Begeisterung und Euphorie bei der Sache, um dieses außergewöhnliche Projekt fertigzustellen. Das Ergebnis zeigt, dass die Umsetzung einer Idee über weite Distanzen mit großem Erfolg möglich ist.

Maria-I. Martín-Peláez[2]

[1] Kengo Kuma & Associates
[2] Hochbauamt Stadt Frankfurt am Main

Gerd Schmid[1]

Modern Teahouse: Form – Structural Analysis – Detail

Modern Teahouse: Form – Statik – Detail

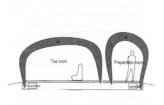

September 2005
September 2005

Introduction

The Modern Teahouse is a project which was first brought to our attention in late 2005; our design work began at the end of 2006 and was completed in ten months. If one were to recreate those ten months in film minutes, one would have seven minutes of quiet opening credits and three minutes of action. During the opening credits there would be flashes of eight variations flickering across the screen and many e-mails in German, English and Japanese: questions and answers would merge into a colorful kaleidoscope. Since the project started out as a nonprofit undertaking, it took a considerable amount of time before the team had established a common goal and before a team structure, financing and division of labor were determined.
Kengo Kuma's earliest sketches already show a double-walled structure with a soft outline, which we continued to modify in monthly discussions, always moving towards greater precision until we arrived at a self-supporting, double-wall inflatable structure with minimal installation and dismantling times — this after a 'detour' which involved a plug-in frame with a membrane shell. The ultimate solution also proved compatible with the budget envisioned by the Japanese patrons and the museum.

In the end we had at our disposal all detachable connection methods such as zippers, screws and sliders and, in particular, air as a load-bearing material and membrane, which served as a tensile building material with maximum compactability.

Einführung

Das Modern Teahouse ist ein Projekt, von dem wir das erste Mal Ende 2005 hörten, dessen Planung für uns Ende 2006 begann und von da an zehn Monate dauerte. Würde man diese zehn Monate in Filmminuten wiedergeben, so erhielte man sieben Minuten ruhiger Vorspann und drei Minuten Action. Im Vorspann würden acht Varianten und viele E-Mails in deutscher, englischer oder japanischer Sprache aufblitzen, Fragen und Antworten würden sich kunterbunt vermischen. Da das Projekt als Non-Profit-Aktion begann, dauerte es entsprechend, bis sich das Team ein gemeinsames Ziel geschaffen hatte und Struktur, Geld und Arbeitsteilung gefunden waren.
Schon die ersten Zeichnungen von Kengo Kuma zeigen einen weich geformten Doppelschalenkörper, den wir in den monatlichen Arbeitsgesprächen modifizierten und so lange präzisierten, bis über den Umweg eines steckbaren Gerüsts mit Membranhülle der selbsttragende Zweiwandpneu mit minimierten Auf- und Abbauzeiten wurde — und der dann auch in das Budget passte, wie es sich die japanischen Förderer und das Museum vorstellten.

Schlussendlich standen uns alle lösbaren Verbindungsmethoden wie Zippen, Schrauben und Einziehen zur Verfügung und vor allem Luft als tragender Baustoff und Membrane, die als zugbeanspruchbarer und maximal kompaktierbarer Werkstoff diente.

February 2006
Februar 2006

¹ formTL ingenieure für tragwerk und leichtbau gmbh

Project description

Thanks to its half peanut shape, the teahouse was soon given the working title 'Peanut': a roughly 80-m^2-large membrane surrounds a roughly 60-m^2-large membrane with a distance of 40 to 100 cm. Both membranes are welded airtight to one another at the installation surface and linked per square meter of surface by four to five thin synthetic cables between which the supporting air is injected — similar to an inflatable boat or a floatation device for swimmers.

However, since the two shells are only partially coupled at specific points, instead following the chamber pattern of an air mattress, for example, the result is a golf ball shape, which defines the texture of the inner and outer surface. The interior pressure creates a flexible shell which transfers loads into two directions. In this "soft shell," the size of the installation surface, the inner pressure and the number of connections are the principal factors for the stability. From 1,000 Pascal upward, the 'peanut' is fully inflated and upright, from 1,500 Pascal onward the soft shell is stable and strong enough to withstand a storm.

The pavilion consists of an autonomous, double-walled shell consisting of an outer and an inner membrane which are connected via many short cables. Despite the use of air as supporting element, this special design does not require air locks because the air pressure inside the pavilion is the same as the air pressure outside of the pavilion. The advantage of this rarely employed building method by comparison to the inflated shed is that it can be installed much more quickly in any location and any condition — in snow or even floating on water.

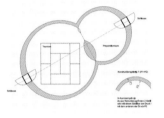

March 2006
März 2006

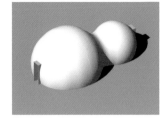

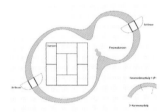

September 2006
September 2006

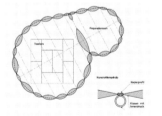

März 2006
March 2006

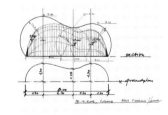

December 2006 sphere generation
Dezember 2006 Kugelgenerierung

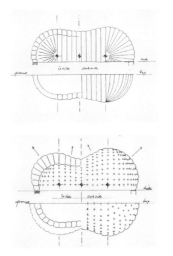

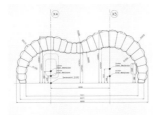

December 2006
Dezember 2006

June 2007 longitudinal section
Juni 2007 Längsschnitt

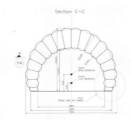

March 2007
März 2007

Coupling cables in transmitted light
Koppelseile im Durchlicht

Projektbeschreibung

Für das Teehaus fand sich wegen seiner halben Erdnussform bald der Arbeitstitel Peanut: Eine etwa 80 Quadratmeter große Membranhülle umschließt mit 40–100 Zentimeter Abstand eine etwa 60 Quadratmeter große Membranhülle. Beide Hüllen sind an der Aufstandsfläche luftdicht miteinander verschweißt und pro Quadratmeter Oberfläche je vier- bis fünfmal mit dünnen Kunststoffseilen gekoppelt, zwischen die dann stützende Luft eingeblasen wird – vergleichbar einem Schlauchboot oder einem Schwimmflügel. Da aber anstelle von Membranstreifen (Schotten) wie bei einer Luftmatratze die beiden Hüllen nur punktweise gekoppelt werden, entsteht ein „Golfball"-Shape, das die Textur der inneren und der äußeren Oberfläche bestimmt. Durch den aufgebrachten Innendruck bildet sich eine biegeweiche Schale, die Lasten in zwei Achsen abträgt. Bei dieser „weichen Schale" bestimmen die Größe der Aufstandsfläche, der Innendruck und die Anzahl der Verknüpfungen maßgeblich die Stabilität. Ab 1000 Pascal Innendruck steht das Peanut auf, und bei 1500 Pascal ist die „weiche Schale" so stabil, dass sie sogar einem Sturm standhält.

Der Pavillon besteht aus einer eigenständigen doppelwandigen Membranhülle, deren äußere und innere Membrane durch viele kurze Seilstücke gekoppelt sind. Trotz Luftstützung werden bei dieser speziellen Ausformung keine Schleusen benötigt, da im Pavillon gewöhnlicher Luftdruck herrscht. Der Vorteil dieser nur selten angewandten Bauweise gegenüber der Traglufthalle: Der Aufbau kann viel schneller erfolgen, und das Objekt kann überall aufgebaut werden – auch auf

The Modern Teahouse is designed as a worry-free structure and able to withstand far greater forces than one might assume at first glance. When the pavilion is set up outside, it can withstand winds of up to 100 km, provided it is anchored on the inside and the outside to a foundation slab with the help of high-performance zippers running around the entire perimeter. For set up in an interior, for example the museum lobby, neither an anchor nor a guide are required — a fact that came as a surprise to us even though the structural model calculations had predicted as much.

Structural analysis

In the pre-tension load analysis (left column), the loads are carried evenly by all building components (inner membrane — coupling cables — outer membrane). Model studies were carried out for two additional types of load: wind coming from the side (lateral wind load) and wind from above (top wind load). In each load case there are noticeable deformations and a new equilibrium between the forces acting on the structure from the outside and the forces resisting from the inside. The colors indicate the tension present in the three building components (green = low tension, yellow = average tension, red = high tension).

The pronounced increases in local forces in the coupling ropes and the membrane under wind pressure or driving rain are especially noticeable, when the pavilion is indented by up to 40 cm in the middle. Since the coupling ropes prevent a separation of the two shells, the compressed air pocket cannot expand and its compression is thus increased.

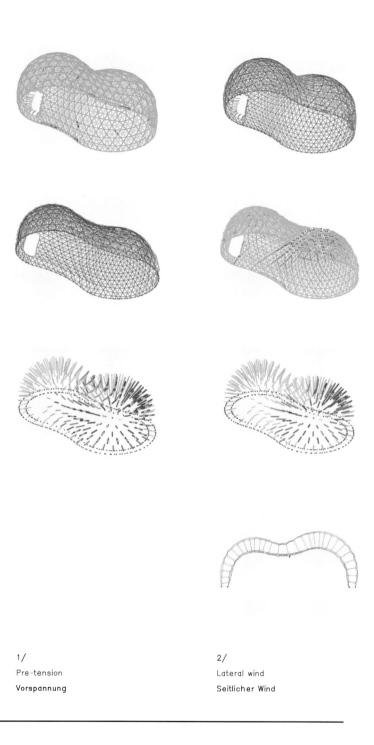

1/

Pre-tension

Vorspannung

2/

Lateral wind

Seitlicher Wind

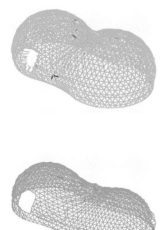

/1

Outer membrane

Äußere Membrane

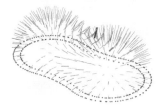

/2

Inner membrane

Innere Membrane

/3

Coupling cables

Koppelseile

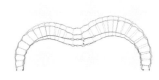

/4

Deformation

Verformung

3/

Wind from above

Wind von oben

Excerpts from structural analyses

Auszüge aus der Statik

Schnee oder sogar schwimmend auf Wasser. Das Modern Teahouse ist als Sorglos-Konstruktion konzipiert und hält weit größeren Kräften stand, als man auf den ersten Blick vermutet. Wird der Pavillon außen aufgebaut, so hält er Wind von bis zu 100 Stundenkilometern aus, sofern er mit innen und außen umlaufenden Hochlastreißverschlüssen auf einer Fundamentplatte verankert wird. Wird es nur im Innenraum, etwa dem Museumsfoyer, aufgebaut, so benötigt es weder eine Verankerung noch eine Führung – was auch uns überraschte, obwohl die modellstatischen Berechnungen dies vorhersagten.

Statik

Im Lastfall Vorspannung (linke Spalte) tragen alle Bauteile (innere Membrane – Koppelseile – äußere Membrane) gleichmäßig. Exemplarisch sind hier zwei weitere Lastfälle untersucht: seitlicher Wind und Wind von oben. Es kommt in jedem der Lastfälle zu deutlichen Formänderungen und einem neuen Kräftegleichgewicht zwischen den von außen einwirkenden Lasten und den von innen dagegen wirkenden Kräften. Die Farben zeigen die Spannungen in den drei Bauteilen (Grün = kleine Spannung, Gelb = mittlere Spannung, Rot = hohe Spannung).

Besonders auffällig sind die lokal stark ansteigenden Kräfte in den Koppelseilen und der Membrane bei Winddruck oder starkem Regen, wenn der Pavillon in der Mitte um bis zu 40 Zentimeter eingedrückt wird. Da die Koppelseile ein Auseinanderdrücken der beiden Hüllen behindern, kann sich das komprimierte Luftpaket nicht weiter ausdehnen und wird dann zusätzlich verdichtet. Hierdurch erhöhen sich lokal die Membranspannungen

This results in a local increase of membrane tension and tensile forces in the coupling cables, activating additional stabilizing elastic forces. This building method owes its structural stability and load-bearing capacity to this "constant volume" principle. However, one requirement resulting from this factor is that the shell must be sufficiently airtight to allow the air pump to continuously refill the space with the amount of compressed supporting air as is escaping at possible leakage points.

Another surprise was that the inner membrane is subjected to greater stresses than the outer membrane (2.0 to 1.5 kN/m) when pre-tensions exist (that is, stresses that are generated wholly by the inner supporting air pressure), while both membranes transfer loads evenly (up to 3.5 kN/m) under wind loads.

Computation program

The membrane shells were analyzed with the help of a program operating with the force-density method, a process of computational modeling for pre-tensioned cables. To this end, the membrane characteristics (stiffness) are imposed on the cables. This program is capable of finding an equilibrium of forces even in strongly deformed systems. To simulate the strongly undulating surface with sufficient accuracy, we used a mesh of only 20 cm edge length for the outer membrane and a mesh of only 15 cm for the inner membrane.

Membrane made of Tenara 3T40

The shells are fashioned from one of the most valuable membrane materials currently available. Manufactured by W. L. Gore & Associates, the fabric material consists of expanded polytetrafluorethylene. Given a thickness of only 0.38 mm and a weight per unit area of 630 g/m^2 it is not only highly transparent (38% transmission in the visible light range), but also capable of withstanding considerable force in both directions, roughly 3000/2900 N/5 cm (that translates into 6 t per meter). Given the pronounced folding resistance and the two- to five-times higher tear resistance by comparison to standard coated fabrics, we anticipate that the structure will hold up very well even after repeated installation and deflation.
The manufacturer recommends 50-mm-wide high-frequency welding seams. With the help of welding and stress tests at the ELLF laboratories (Essener Labor für Leichte Flächentragwerke), we were able to determine that 30-mm-wide seams are sufficient for the tensions occurring with this structure; this solution also presents an advantage with regard to the intricate pattern. At 23 degrees, the 30-mm seams can withstand 1400 N/5 cm. At 70 degrees, this value drops to 900 N/5 cm as a result of the heat-sensitive seams (Thermoplast). The stress of 1,500 Pascal of interior pressure, relevant for the calculations in this case, lies at roughly 175 N/5 cm and corresponds to standard safety factors for membrane structures.

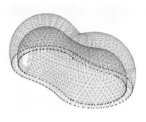

Structural model wall with all spare rods
Statikmodell mit allen Ersatzstäben

70

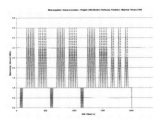

Biaxial test parameters
Biaxialtestvorgabe

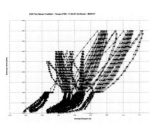

Biaxial test results
Biaxialtestergebnisse

und die Zugkräfte in den Koppelseilen, so dass zusätzlich stabilisierende Rückstellkräfte aktiviert werden. Diesem Prinzip des „Constanl Volume" verdankt diese Bauweise ihre Stabilität und Tragfähigkeit.

Das heißt aber auch, dass die Hülle so luftdicht sein muss, dass das Stützluftaggregat stets so viel komprimierte Stützluft nachfüllen kann, wie an irgendwelchen Leckstellen entweicht.

Überraschend war auch, dass im Lastfall Vorspannung (Spannungen, die nur durch den inneren Stützluftdruck entstehen) die innere Membrane stärker beansprucht wird als die äußere Membrane (2,0 zu 1,5 kN/m), während sich bei Wind beide Membranen gleich stark mit bis 3,5 kN/m am Lastabtrag beteiligen.

Rechenprogramm

Die Membranhüllen sind mit Hilfe eines Programms untersucht worden, das mit der Kraft-Dichte-Methode arbeitet, bei der die Membranen als Seilmodell mit Vierecksmaschen abstrahiert werden. Dazu werden den Seilen die Membraneigenschaften (Steifigkeit) eingeprägt. Dieses Programm findet selbst an sehr stark verformten Systemen ein Kräftegleichgewicht. Um die stark ondulierte Oberfläche hinreichend exakt zu simulieren, haben wir für die äußere Membrane ein Netz mit nur 20 Zentimetern Kantenlänge und für die innere Membrane mit 15 Zentimetern Kantenlänge verwendet.

Membrane aus Tenara 3T40

Die Hüllen sind aus einem der hochwertigsten Membranmaterialen gefertigt, die derzeit verfügbar sind. Es handelt sich um ein Gewebe aus Flurkunststofffasern im Verbund mit Flurfolien und stammt von W.L. Gore & Associates. Bei nur 0,38 Millimeter und einem Flächengewicht von 630 g/m^2 ist es nicht nur sehr lichtdurchlässig (38 Prozent Transmission im Bereich des sichtbaren Lichts), sondern mit ca. 3000/2900 N/5cm (das sind 6 to pro Meter) in beide Richtungen besonders belastbar. Wir erwarten wegen der ausgeprägten Knickunempfindlichkeit und der zwei- bis fünffach besseren Weiterreißfestigkeit gegenüber herkömmlich beschichteten Geweben eine besonders lange Haltbarkeit auch bei vielfachem Auf- und Abbauen.

Der Hersteller empfiehlt 50 Millimeter breite Hochfrequenz-Schweißnähte. Wir haben mit Hilfe von Schweiß- und Zugversuchen am Essener Labor für Leichte Flächentragwerke (ELLF) ermittelt, dass 30 Millimeter breite Nähte für die hier auftretenden Spannungen ausreichen, was auch im Layout besser zu dem kleinteiligen Zuschnitt passt. Die Schweißnähte von 30 Millimetern halten bei 23 Grad 1400 N/5 cm. Dieser Wert reduziert sich aufgrund der wärmeempfindlichen Nähte (Thermoplast) bei 70 Grad auf 900 N/5 cm. Die hier bemessungsrelevante Beanspruchung mit 1500 Pascal Innendruck liegt bei 175 N/5 cm und entspricht gängigen Sicherheitsfaktoren bei Membranbauten.

Cutting pattern, seam layout, connections, details, manufacture

The fabric is 1.5 m wide and was halved by us for the cutting pattern to ensure that the small radii of curvature, which the computational models revealed between the coupling cables in the two membranes, could form without wrinkles.

The two 80 and 60 square meter membranes consist of 116 pieces, excluding the door openings and the cable connectors. The individual membrane pieces are only 0.2 to 3.5 square meters in size (approx. 1.2 square meters on average) and highly labor intensive to manufacture and finish.

The two membranes are combined into a supporting unit by coupling 306 synthetic cables with spring safety hooks, each 40 to 80 cm long, through the welded door openings and the surrounding welded base membrane. For maintenance and repair purposes two airtight, 1.5-m-long Tizip-zippers have been integrated in the base membrane, the only stitched position and air leakage zone as a result of the material incompatibility of PVC and Tenara.

The quasi perpendicular connection of the two shells required special attention, which was only approximately possible since the inner and outer membrane are geometrically "dissimilar" (similar forms result from scaling a basic form). Additionally, we had to integrate 306 welding positions precisely for the individual membrane pieces and establish clear allocations for 306 cables of differing length. Canobbio S.p.A., a highly professional expert manufacturer in northern Italy, gathered a 15-person crew in his 6,000 square meter workshop in Castelnuovo, which assumed the complicated task to finishing the fabric pattern. Given the modest size of the pavilion and the low pre-tensioning of the pavilion membranes, the work had to meet extraordinarily high standards of precision because any inaccuracies and folds would be visible later on. The effort in labor per square meter was three times by comparison to other membrane structures because every element of this pavilion is on a smaller scale and visible from up close.

We had always been aware that form, material and structural integrity were as one in this project and that we could not afford to make any compromises. An important factor was that Canobbio tested our details and optimized them until Signor Bargelli, technician of the production, was also satisfied. The cone-shaped cut of the welding positions, which prevents any wrinkles in the outer membranes, deserves special mention because this area was especially vulnerable to wrinkles due to the localized load transfer of the cables.

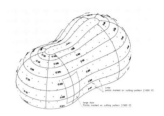

Pattern overview 3-D
Zuschnittsübersicht 3-D

Welding a straplink fastener
Aufschweißen des Straplink-Befestigungspunkts

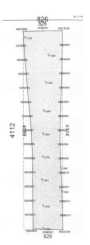

Two-dimensional layout of section
3/4 of the outer membrane
Verebneter Zuschnitt von Bahn
3/4 der äußeren Membrane

Fastener and straplink
Befestigungspunkt und Straplink

Zuschnitt, Nahtlayout, Verbindungen, Details, Konfektion

Das Gewebe liegt 1,5 Meter breit und wurde von uns für die Zuschnitte nochmals halbiert, damit die kleinen Krümmungsradien, die sich zwischen den Koppelseilen in den beiden Hüllen rechnerisch einstellen, faltenfrei ausformen können.
Die beiden 80 und 60 Quadratmeter großen Hüllen bestehen aus 116 Membranstücken, die Türausschnitte und die vielteiligen Seilverbinder-Anschlussteller nicht eingerechnet. Die Membranstücke sind lediglich 0,2 bis 3,5 Quadratmeter groß, im Mittel etwa 1,2 Quadratmeter, und sehr verarbeitungsintensiv.

Zur tragenden Einheit werden beide Hüllen durch die Kopplung über 306 Kunststoffseile mit schraubbaren Karabinerhaken, je 40 bis 80 Zentimeter lang, durch die eingeschweißten Türausschnitte und die umlaufend eingeschweißte Fußmembrane. Zu Revisionszwecken sind außerdem zwei luftdichte, je 1,5 Meter lange Tizip-Reißverschlüsse in die Fußmembrane integriert, was aufgrund der Materialinkompatibilität von PVC und Tenara die einzige genähte Position und Luft-Leckzone ist. Besonderes Augenmerk benötigte die quasi normale Verbindung beider Hüllen, was nur in etwa möglich war, da die innere und die äußere Hülle geometrisch „nicht ähnlich" sind (ähnliche Formen entstehen durch

Skalieren einer Grundform). Außerdem galt es, je 306 Aufschweißpunkte lagerichtig auf die Zuschnittsbahnen zu integrieren und eine eindeutige Zuordnung zu 306 Seilstücken unterschiedlicher Länge herzustellen.

Der leistungsstarke norditalienische Konfektionär Canobbio S.p.A. hat in seinem 6000 Quadratmeter großen Werk in Castelnouvo eine 15-köpfige Crew zusammengestellt, die sich um die sehr komplizierte Fertigung kümmerte. Auf Grund der geringen Größe des Pavillons und der geringen Vorspannung der Membranen des Pavillons musste über die Maßen genau gearbeitet werden, denn Maßungenauigkeiten und Falten werden später sichtbar sein. Der Arbeitsaufwand pro Quadratmeter betrug das Dreifache üblicher Membrankonstruktionen, weil alles an diesem Pavillon kleinteilig und aus direkter Nähe sichtbar ist.

Uns war stets bewusst, dass hier die Form, das Material und die Statik eins waren und wir keine Kompromisse eingehen durften. Wichtig war, dass Canobbio unsere Details testete und so lange optimierte, bis auch Fertigungsleiter Signore Bargelli damit zufrieden war. Besonders erwähnenswert ist der nunmehr konische Zuschnitt der Aufschweißpunkte, die jegliche Falten in der Außenhülle vermeidet, obwohl gerade hier durch die lokale Lasteinleitung der Seile Falten zu befürchten waren.

Foundation slab and LED channel

To ensure that the pavilion won't be taken away by the wind, 2 tons of uplifting must be braced along the outer attachment line and 1 ton along the inner attachment line. Localized, this translates into 150 kg per meter. To this end, the pavilion is fastened inside and outside with 40 high-performance zippers (30 kN/m load-bearing capacity) to the light transmitters that are integrated in the extruded keder profiles. The latter are bolted with resin anchors to the kidney-shaped foundation slab.

Air management

An "oversized" air aggregate ensures rapid inflation times of only ten minutes. The 1.5 kilowatt strong radial-flow compressor delivers 1,000 cubic meters at a pressure of up to 2,200 Pascal. To prevent humidity or dirt from accumulating in the membrane interior, the air is suctioned in via fine dust filters and dehumidified with the help of a 0.9 kilowatt absorption drier.

Following a test installation in the outside, two operating methods were tested in the lobby of the museum: sequential and sliding operation. Sequential operation allows for the temporary shut down of the aggregates, albeit at the cost of noisy "catch-up" sounds when the aggregate is switched on again. Sliding operation turned out to be far more agreeable: with this operating method, leakages are constantly compensated on a steady but minute scale. Hence the air compressor can be set up and operated in the lobby without causing any nuisance.

The blower and the drier as well as a small 0.6 kilowatt suction fan (for rapid deflation and disassembly) are built into a waffle-baffled steel box on balloon tires, which can be easily moved by two people.

Dimensions

Floor area: 32 square meters
Edge: 20 meters
Cushion volume: 35 cubic meters
Principal measurements: 9 m x 4.6 m x 3.4 m (length x width x height)

Companies and planning consultants

Client: Museum of Applied Arts Frankfurt, Prof. Schneider

Concept and architectural design: KKAA Kengo Kuma & Associates, Tōkyō, Japan
Supervision: Building Department of the City of Frankfurt

Structural engineers:
formTL ingenieure für tragwerk und leichtbau gmbH Radolfzell
- Design, details, tender documents, technical supervision:
  Dipl.-Ing. Architekt Gerd Schmid
- Form development, structural analysis, pattern design: Dipl.-Ing. Gerhard Fessler
- Form development pattern:
  Dipl.-Ing. Bernd Stimpfle
- Workshop drawings:
  Udo Ribbe, Manuel Neidhart
- Manufacture and installation:
  Canobbio S.p.A., Castelnouvo (I)
- Mobile air supply: S+H Nolting GmbH, Detmold

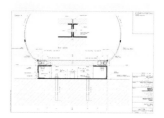

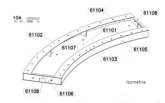

Box groove
Kastenrinne

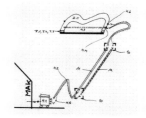

Hose diagram
Leitungsführung

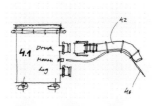

Compressed air aggregate
Stützluftaggregat

isometric view

The main compressed air connection was
manufactured specifically for this project
Der Stützluft-Hauptanschluss ist eigens für
dieses Projekt gefertigt worden

For the hoses (DN75, pressure- and suction-
proof, polyurethane with spiral insert) and
fittings, robust and functional components
from the food industry were utilized.
Bei Schläuchen (DN75, druck- und sogfest
aus PU mit Spiraleinlage) und Armaturen
wurde auf robuste und funktionelle Bauteile
aus der Lebensmittelindustrie zurückgegriffen.

Bodenplatte und LED-Rinne

Damit der Pavillon vom Wind nicht weg-
getragen wird, müssen entlang der äußeren
Befestigungslinie 2 Tonnen abhebende
Kräfte und an der inneren Befestigungslinie
1 Tonne verankert werden. Das sind lokal
bis zu 150 Kilogramm pro Meter. Der Pavillon
ist deshalb umlaufend innen und außen mit
40 Schwerlastreißverschlüssen (30 kN/m
Tragkraft) auf den Lichtträgern befestigt,
die in Kedernutprofile eingezogen sind.
Diese wiederum sind mit Klebeankern auf
der nierenförmigen Betonplatte verschraubt.

Stützluftmanagement

Für sehr kurze Aufblaszeiten von nur 10
Minuten sorgt ein „überdimensioniertes"
Stützluftaggregat. Der 1,5 Kilowatt starke
Radiallüfter liefert 1000 Kubikmeter mit bis
zu 2200 Pascal Druck. Damit sich im Inneren
der Hülle keine Feuchtigkeit oder Schmutz
niederschlägt, wird die Luft über Feinstaub-
filter angesaugt und mit einem 0,9 Kilowatt
starken Absorbtionstrockner entfeuchtet.
Im Foyer des Museums wurden im Anschluss
an den Probeaufbau draußen zwei Betriebs-
arten getestet: sequenzieller und gleitender
Betrieb. Der sequenzielle Betrieb erlaubt ein
zeitweises Abschalten der Aggregate, was
aber mit lauten „Aufholgeräuschen" beim
Anschalten verbunden ist. Als wesentlich
angenehmer zeigte sich der gleitende Betrieb,
bei dem ständig, dafür aber auf niedrigem
Niveau, Leckagen ausgeglichen werden.
Das Stützluftgerät kann deshalb problemlos
im Foyer stehen und betrieben werden.
Das Druckgebläse und der Trockner sowie

ein kleineres Sauggebläse mit 0,6 Kilowatt
(für eine schnelle Demontage) sind in eine
waffelgedämmte Stahlbox auf Luftbereifung
eingebaut, die von zwei Personen bewegt
werden kann.

Maße

Grundfläche: 32 Quadratmeter
Randlänge: 20 Meter
Kissenvolumen: 35 Kubikmeter
Hauptmaße: 9 m x 4,6 m x 3,4 m
(Länge x Breite x Höhe)

Firmen und Planer

Bauherr: Museum für Angewandte Kunst
Frankfurt, Prof. Schneider

Idee und Architektur: KKAA Kengo Kuma &
Associates, Tōkyō, Japan
Bauleitung: Hochbauamt Stadt Frankfurt

Tragwerksplanung:
formTL ingenieure für tragwerk und
leichtbau gmbH Radolfzell
- Entwurf, Details, Ausschreibung,
  Fachbauleitung:
  Dipl.-Ing. Architekt Gerd Schmid
- Formfindung Statik, Zuschnitte:
  Dipl.-Ing. Gerhard Fessler
- Formfindung Zuschnitt:
  Dipl.-Ing. Bernd Stimpfle
- Werkstattzeichnungen:
  Udo Ribbe, Manuel Neidhart
- Konfektion und Montage:
  Canobbio S.p.A., Castelnouvo (I)
- Mobile Stützluftversorgung:
  S+H Nolting GmbH, Detmold

Stephan Graf von der Schulenburg
Teatime

If man were never to fade away like the dews of Adashino, never to vanish like the smoke over Toribeyama, but lingered on forever in this world, how things would lose their power to move us! The most precious thing in life is its uncertainty.
Yoshida Kenkō[1]

"Pavilion of waves in moonlight" (Geppa-rō) in the gardens of the Katsura Palace near Kyōto, erected in the 1620s by Prince Toshihito. The simple building, which adheres to a rural style, features a balcony that was designed specifically for contemplating the moonlight and its reflection on the water

„Pavillon der Wellen im Mondschein" (Geppa-rō) im Garten des Katsura-Palastes bei Kyōto, errichtet in den 1620er Jahren von Prinz Toshihito. Das schlichte, im ländlichen Stil gehaltene Gebäude verfügt über einen Balkon, der eigens zur Betrachtung des Mondlichts und seiner Spiegelung im Wasser errichtet wurde

The word "tea" is one of the few basic expressions of human civilization that sound identical or at least similar in nearly all world languages — "cha" in China, Korea, Japan and Persia, "chai" in Hindi, Russian and Bulgarian, "shai" in Arabic and "Tee", "tea," "thé" or similar in nearly all western and central European languages. In the west, the word tea may at first conjure up images of formal British afternoon parties, of Meißner porcelain or the Boston Tea Party, which gave momentum to the struggle for independence in the United States of America, perhaps even of Leonard Cohen and his ballad of the mysteriously beautiful Suzanne, who enhances her charms with tea and oranges. At the same time, among westerners, tea is also synonymous with the wisdom and profundity of Asia's ancient cultures. In this capacity tea — in particular unfermented green tea — has become a fashionable beverage worldwide. Countless reports on the many different therapeutic properties of the tea plant also play a role in this development. Thus a chic bistro in downtown Frankfurt is called "Teelirium": here tea is celebrated as a lifestyle drink.[2] The 26-page tea menu at the establishment offers standard fare such as Darjeeling or plain Japanese *sencha* as well as mysterious beverages like the "Orient Express" — a mix of black and green tea with jackfruit-

If man were never to fade away like the dews of Adashino, never to vanish like the smoke over Toribeyama, but lingered on forever in this world, how things would lose their power to move us! The most precious thing in life is its uncertainty.
Yoshida Kenkō[1]

Das Wort „Tee" gehört zu den wenigen Grundbegriffen der menschlichen Zivilisation, die in beinahe allen Weltsprachen gleich oder zumindest ähnlich klingen — „cha" in China, Korea, Japan und Persien, „chai" in Hindi, Russisch und Bulgarisch, „shai" im Arabischen und „Tee", „tea", „thé" oder ähnlich in fast allen west- und mitteleuropäischen Sprachen. Im Westen denkt man beim Begriff Tee vielleicht zunächst an steife britische Nachmittagsgesellschaften, an Meißner Porzellan, an die Boston Tea Party, mit der der Freiheitskampf der Vereinigten Staaten an Fahrt gewann, vielleicht sogar an Leonard Cohen, der die geheimnisvolle schöne Suzanne besingt, die ihre körperlichen Reize mit Tee und Orangen unterstreicht. Zugleich steht der Tee auch bei uns Westlern für die Weisheit und die Tiefe der alten Kulturen Asiens. In dieser Eigenschaft ist Tee, zumal der unfermentierte grüne Tee, in den letzten Jahren weltweit zu einer Art Modegetränk geworden. Hier spielen auch zahlreiche Berichte über die vielfältige Heilwirkung der Teepflanze eine Rolle. „Teelirium" etwa nennt sich ein schickes Bistro in der Frankfurter Innenstadt, in dem Tee als Lifestyle-Getränk zelebriert wird.[2] Die 26-seitige Teekarte des Hauses bietet neben regulärem Darjeeling oder schlichtem japanischem *sencha* auch geheimnisvolle Getränke wie „Orientexpress" — schwarzer und grüner Tee gemischt und

[1] Essays in Idleness. The Tsurezuregusa of Kenkō. Translated by Donald Keene. New York/London: Columbia University Press 1967, p. 7. The Japanese original was first published between 1330 and 1332. In this essay historic Japanese names up to the end of the feudal era in 1868 are rendered according to the standard Japanese convention of given name followed by the surname.
[2] Cf.: www.teelirium.de.

[1] Essays in Idleness. The Tsurezuregusa of Kenkō. Translated by Donald Keene. New York/London: Columbia University Press 1967, S. 7. Das japanische Original erschien zwischen 1330 und 1332. Historische japanische Namen bis zum Ende der Feudalzeit 1868 werden in diesem Aufsatz in der in Japan üblichen Reihenfolge Vorname vor Familienname wiedergegeben.
[2] Vgl.: www.teelirium.de.

peach-vanilla flavor, sunflower blossoms, rose blossoms and aromatics (at Euro 4,90 a pot). Patrons can also order a *"matcha*[3] kiwi latte" — a combination that would make any friend of the Japanese tea ceremony run for the hills!

The current tea craze around the world is no doubt at least in part responsible for the multifaceted renaissance that tea is also experiencing in its region of origin, East Asia. There is the Wisteria Tea House in Taipei, run by a tea merchant and scholar, a meeting place for the democratic movement, the art scene and the intelligentsia of the city for as far back as the 1960s. In contemporary China, teahouses are once again an everyday part of urban culture and South Korea is also in the process of rediscovering a specifically Korean tea culture.[4] But the country that gained the greatest fame even beyond its own borders as a land known for its unique celebration of "The Way of Tea" is Japan.

However, before turning our attention towards tea and the tea ceremony in Japan, I would like to briefly describe how I came to know this beverage myself. I was a teenager and used to love listening to Leonard Cohen's "Suzanne." For as long as I can remember, my parents owned a red English crockery tea pot, the kind that is still for sale in nearly all tea stores. When my father — who never did anything in the kitchen — brewed tea, we witnessed a kind of ritual, a tea ceremony so to speak albeit far removed from the rigorous rules of the Japanese tea ceremony. First he would rinse out the pot with hot water so that it would be prewarmed when he poured in boiling water for tea. The staple was Earl Grey taken from a pale blue,

square tin, a black Indian tea with the characteristic bergamot oil aroma. Sometimes, the tea-drinking ritual could take on astonishing traits, when my father, my mother, my brother and I might depart at the end of a summer's day of work, around five or six o'clock in the evening, with a tray bearing the large red tea pot, cups, plates and some baked goods and wander into the small park-like forest near our house. Our destination was a slab of rock above a small river — an ideal spot to settle down and wait for the sunset while sipping on a cup of tea.

The deep connection to drinking tea has stayed with me ever since. I have drunk tea in all situations of life and always experienced a specific, stimulating and alert sense of contentment — as I am in this very moment while writing these lines. Around 1980, when the eco-movement was just beginning to take off in Europe, I discovered the "Projektwerkstatt Teekampagne," a project initiated by the Freie University of Berlin, derided by some at the time, which focused on fair trade, transparency in international trade and pesticide-free tea cultivation in the Himalayas.[5] To this day, tea time is held everyday at lunch, a much-loved tradition among all of us in the Museum of Applied Arts, incidentally still tea from this importer, who hails from Darjeeling, one of the best tea-growing areas in the world. One small difference is that today, unfermented, green tea is also cultivated in that region, a type of tea that is mainly common in East Asia.

All this, however, has little relation to the role which tea drinking has played in Japan since the sixteenth century. One might well

Interiors of the En'an teahouse — view of the *tokonoma* and (to the right) the host's entrance and the area for tea preparation. This tearoom was designed by Furuta Oribe (1544-1615), restored in 1830-35 and transferred to its present location, the Yabunouchi School of Tea in Kyōto in 1867.

Innenansichten des En'an-Teehauses — Blick auf die *tokonoma* und (rechts) den Eingang für den Gastgeber und Platz zum Anrichten des Tees.
Dieser Teeraum wurde entworfen von Furuta Oribe (1544-1615), 1830-35 restauriert und 1867 an seinen heutigen Ort transferiert, die Yabunouchi-Teeschule in Kyōto

---

[3] *Matcha* is the name of the finely pulverized, concentrated green tea used in the Japanese tea ceremony.
[4] Cf. Yoo Yang-Seok: The Book of Korean Tea. A Guide to the History, Culture and Philosophy of Korean Tea and the Tea Ceremony. Seoul: The Myung Won Cultural Foundation, 2007.
[5] The high quality and favorable prices helped Berlin's "Teekampagne" to grow into Germany's largest tea import company within a few short years.

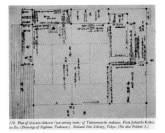

110. Plan of chatate-dokoro (tea-serving room) of Takinomoto-bo teahouse. From Juhachi Kakoi no Zu (Drawings of Eighteen Teahouses). National Diet Library, Tokyo. (See also Foldout 2.)

Historic plan of a teahouse:
Plan of the *chatate-dokoro*, the room in which tea is served, for the Takinomoto-bō Teahouse. In: Jūhachi kakoi no zu ("Plans for Eighteen Teahouses"), National Diet Library, Tōkyō
Historischer Plan eines Teehauses:
Plan des *chatate-dokoro*, des Raums zum Servieren des Tees, für das Takinomoto-bō Teehaus. Aus: Jūhachi kakoi no zu ("Pläne für achtzehn Teehäuser"), National Diet Library, Tōkyō

mit Jackfruit-Pfirsich-Vanille-Geschmack, Sonnenblumenblüten, Rosenblüten und Aromastoffen (das Kännchen zu 4,90 Euro). Bestellen kann man auch „matcha[3] Kiwi Latte". Eine Kombination wie diese würde jeden japanischen Freund der Teezeremonie das Fürchten lehren!

Vermutlich ist der derzeit weltweit zu beobachtende Tee-Boom mit dafür verantwortlich, dass auch in der historischen Ursprungsregion des Tees, in Ostasien, die Teekultur eine vielfältige Renaissance erlebt. Da gibt es das von einem Teehändler und Gelehrten betriebene Wistaria Tea House in Taipeh, wo sich bereits seit den 60er Jahren die Demokratiebewegung, die kritische Kunstszene und ganz allgemein die Intelligenzija der Stadt trifft. Auch in der Volksrepublik China gehören Teehäuser heute wieder selbstverständlich zur städtischen Kultur, und in Südkorea wird zurzeit die spezifisch koreanische Teekultur wieder entdeckt.[4] Das Land aber, das auch über die eigenen Grenzen hinaus am meisten für seinen besonderen Tee-Weg bekannt wurde, ist Japan.

Doch bevor wir uns dem Tee und der Teezeremonie in Japan zuwenden, möchte ich kurz schildern, wie ich selbst dieses Getränk kennen gelernt habe. Ich war ein Teenager, und ich hörte damals besonders gern Leonard Cohens Lied „Suzanne". So lange ich denken kann, besaßen meine Eltern eine rote englische Steinzeug-Teekanne, wie sie heute noch in fast jedem Teeladen angeboten wird. Wenn mein Vater, der sonst nie etwas in der Küche tat, den Tee aufbrühte, dann war das so etwas wie ein Ritual, gewissermaßen eine Teezeremonie, wenn auch fern von den strengen Regeln des

japanischen Teezeremoniells. Es begann damit, dass er die Kanne heiß ausspülte, damit diese vorgewärmt war, wenn er das heiße Wasser aufgoss. Verwendung fand stets Earl Grey aus einer hellblauen, würfelförmigen Blechdose, also ein indischer schwarzer Tee mit charakteristischem Bergamottöl-Aroma. Das Ritual des Teetrinkens nahm zeitweise erstaunliche Züge an, wenn mein Vater, meine Mutter, mein Bruder und ich im Sommer nach der Arbeit des Tages, also gegen fünf oder sechs Uhr abends, die große rote Teekanne, Tassen, Teller und etwas Gebäck auf ein Tablett packten und damit in den kleinen, parkartigen Wald nahe unserem Haus aufbrachen. Ziel dieser Prozession war eine Felsplatte über einem kleinen Fluss – ein idealer Standort, um hier bei einer Tasse Tee den Sonnenuntergang abzuwarten.

Die tiefe Verbundenheit mit dem Teetrinken hat mich seither begleitet. In allen Lebenslagen habe ich Tee getrunken und dabei eine spezifische, angeregt-wache Zufriedenheit empfunden – wie auch jetzt, während ich diese Zeilen schreibe. Um 1980, zur Zeit der aufkeimenden Ökobewegung in Europa, entdeckte ich die „Projektwerkstatt Teekampagne", ein damals noch zum Teil belächeltes Projekt der Freien Universität Berlin, bei dem es um Fair Trade, Transparenz im internationalen Handel und die Vermeidung von Spritzmitteln beim Teeanbau im Himalaya ging.[5] Und noch heute, im Museum für Angewandte Kunst, findet täglich um die Mittagszeit eine uns allen lieb gewordene Teestunde statt, übrigens noch immer mit dem Tee des oben vorgestellten Importeurs, der aus Darjeeling stammt, einem der besten Teeanbaugebiete der Welt. Ein kleiner Unterschied ist, dass dort heute auch unfermen-

---

[3] Als *matcha* wird der fein pulverisierte grüne Tee für die japanische Teezeremonie bezeichnet.
[4] Vgl. Yoo Yang-Seok: The Book of Korean Tea. A Guide to the History, Culture and Philosophy of Korean Tea and the Tea Ceremony. Seoul: The Myung Won Cultural Foundation, 2007.
[5] Die hohe Qualität und der günstige Einkaufspreis ließ die Berliner „Teekampagne" schon nach wenigen Jahren zum größten Teeimporteur Deutschlands werden.

pose the question: How should a teahouse built from manmade materials by a renowned contemporary architect in the park of a Frankfurt museum function? No doubt, this project must be seen as an open-ended experiment. And no doubt, Japan can once again portray itself as a land of surprises and innovations with this ephemeral structure — as "Japan the Cool," if you will; incidentally, drawing a clear distinction to two other Frankfurt locales, the picturesque Chinese garden in the Bethmannpark (since 1989) and the Korean garden in the Grüneburgpark (a relatively recent cultural landmark of East Asia's third largest economy). Kengo Kuma's teahouse is indeed much more than a folkloristic display of an ancient culture at the opposite end of the Eurasian landmass. It is an open site with sufficient space to accommodate a variety of projects. What a fortuitous circumstance that one of contemporary Japan's most innovative architects has been won for this project in the person of Kengo Kuma. Yet another manifestation of the future viability of a country which had been plunged into a strange silence in the face of (South) Korea's rapid economic growth and China's breathtaking economic boom.

To understand the project that has been created here in a deeper sense one has to take a closer look at the tea culture in ancient Japan: noblemen and monks drank tea in Japan as early as the eighth century. Like most achievements of civilization this, too, arrived by way of the Asian continent where tea had already been cultivated in the mountainous regions of southern China and Southeast Asia for a long time. Still, several centuries passed before Sen no Rikyū (1522-1591) developed the principles of the tea ceremony as a certain way of life and with it a highly complex, specifically Japanese culture of drinking tea. Rikyū's downright revolutionary achievement was the radical simplification of the tea ceremony, of removing from it all pomp and circumstance. For in the sixteenth century, tea ceremonies had become a political event, a cultural spectacle so to speak, by means of which the powerful sought to gain favor with their vassals and thus strengthen their sphere of influence. Rikyū himself enjoyed the protection of the most powerful man in Japan at the time, the warlord Toyotomi Hideyoshi (1537-1598), and was therefore forced time and again to participate in this kind of display of power. In his novel "Honkakubō ibun" (Death of the Tea Master), the great Japanese writer Inoue Yasushi (1907-1991) describes just such a gathering:

"On the third [day] of the new year, Taikō Hideyoshi held a [...] splendid tea ceremony. [...] Everything was harmonized down to the minutest detail with the decoration of the *tokonoma*. Needless to say that the tea settings in front of the three masters bore only the finest of paraphernalia. The guests were hard pressed to match the magnificence and exquisite taste. After the objects had been viewed and appreciated, a meal was served, which led to a commotion due to the great number of guests. [...] Amidst all this activity, the Taikō was the most striking presence."[6]
The ambivalent attitude of Sen no Rikyū and even of the unscrupulous warlord Hideyoshi vis-à-vis this pomp is all too clearly revealed a few lines later, when the author writes:

[6] Inoue Yasushi: The Death of the Tea Master. (Original Japanese edition published in 1981), here p. 123. Inoue wrote this novel, which is widely regarded as his artistic legacy, on the basis of the first-hand account of one of Rikyū's students, Honkakubō.

Niki Club, Nasu, Prov. Tochigi
Architect: Takeshi Sugimoto + Akira
Watanabe Architect & Associates, 1997
Exterior (left hand page) and view into
interior
Niki Club, Nasu, Prov. Tochigi
Architekt: Takeshi Sugimoto + Akira
Watanabe Architect & Associates, 1997
Außenansicht (linke Seite) und Blick ins
Innere

tierter, grüner Tee angebaut wird, wie er
vornehmlich in Ostasien verbreitet ist.
Doch all dies hat eher wenig mit der Rolle
zu tun, die das Teetrinken in Japan seit
dem 16. Jahrhundert spielt. Es mag berechtigt
sein, sich die Frage zu stellen: Wie soll ein
Kunststoff-Teehaus eines angesehenen
japanischen Gegenwartsarchitekten im Park
eines Frankfurter Museums funktionieren?
Ganz sicher ist dieses Projekt als ein
Experiment mit offenem Ende zu betrachten.
Und zweifellos kann sich Japan mit dieser
ephemeren Architektur einmal mehr als
Land der Überraschungen, der Innovation
präsentieren – als „cool Japan", wenn Sie
so wollen; dies übrigens auch in klarer
Abgrenzung zu zwei anderen Frankfurter Orten,
dem seit 1989 bestehenden, pittoresken
chinesischen Garten im Bethmannpark und
dem koreanischen Garten im Grüneburgpark
als relativ neue Kulturvertretung der dritten
großen Wirtschaftsmacht Ostasiens. Kengo
Kumas Teehaus ist in der Tat viel mehr als
folkloristische Selbstdarstellung einer alten
Kultur am anderen Ende der eurasischen
Landmasse. Es ist ein offener Ort, der vielerlei
Projekten Raum bieten kann. Sicherlich
ist es ein glücklicher Umstand, dass mit
Kengo Kuma einer der innovativsten Architekten des heutigen Japan für dieses
Projekt gewonnen werden konnte. Einmal
mehr manifestiert sich hier die Zukunfts-
fähigkeit eines Landes, um das es in den ver-
gangenen Jahren angesichts der Aufholjagd
(Süd-)Koreas und des atemberaubenden
Wirtschaftsbooms in China merkwürdig still
geworden war.

Um das, was hier entstanden ist, in einem
tieferen Sinne zu verstehen, ist es nötig,
einen genaueren Blick auf die Teekultur im
alten Japan zu werfen: Bereits im 8. Jahrhundert n. Chr. tranken Adelige und Mönche in
Japan Tee. Wie die meisten zivilisatorischen
Errungenschaften kam auch diese vom
asiatischen Festland – schon viel früher war
Tee in den Bergregionen Südchinas und
Südostasiens angebaut worden. Doch es
vergingen noch viele Jahrhunderte, bis Sen
no Rikyū (1522-1591) die Grundlagen für
den Teeweg als Lebensstil und damit eine
hochkomplexe, spezifisch japanische
Kultur des Teetrinkens entwickelte. Rikyūs
geradezu revolutionäre Leistung war es, die
Teezeremonie radikal zu vereinfachen, ihr
allen Pomp und äußerlichen Glanz zu nehmen.
Denn im 16. Jahrhundert waren Teezusam-
menkünfte zu einem Politikum geworden,
gewissermaßen zu einem Kulturspektakel,
mit dem die Mächtigen ihre Vasallen für
sich gewinnen und damit ihre Einflusssphäre
stärken wollten. Rikyū selbst stand unter der
Protektion des damals mächtigsten Mannes
in Japan, des Emporkömmlings Toyotomi
Hideyoshi (1537-1598), und war somit
immer wieder gezwungen, diese Art von
Showveranstaltung mitzumachen. In seinem
Roman „Honkakubō ibun" („Der Tod des
Teemeisters") beschreibt der große japanische
Schriftsteller Inoue Yasushi (1907-1991)
eine derartige Zusammenkunft:

„Eine [...] glanzvolle Teezeremonie veranstal-
tete Taikō Hideyoshi am Dritten des neuen
Jahres. [...] Alles war bis ins Feinste auf die
Dekoration des *tokonoma* abgestimmt.
Unnötig zu erwähnen, dass sich auf den
Teegestellen vor den drei Meistern nur die
vornehmsten Gerätschaften reihten. Nur
schwerlich vermochten die Gäste diese
Pracht und den erlesenen Geschmack zu
übertreffen.

"It's only an assumption but I believe that he invited Hideyoshi on the very same day to a simple and strict ceremony in the Yamazatoan teahouse, covering the area of two *tatami* mats, which he had erected especially for Master Rikyū. In this manner, the Taikō was undoubtedly an outstanding connoisseur of the tea ceremony and knew better than most to appreciate the relaxed atmosphere of the Yamazatoan and Myōkian teahouses."[7]

On the one hand, this turn of events reveals the two-faced character of Hideyoshi's personality, who — as a politician — employed the tea ceremony as a demonstration of power, while regarding it privately very much as a meditative act, entirely in the spirit of the master Sen no Rikyū. At the same time, this excerpt demonstrates how much power the tea master truly had over the most powerful man of the state. Whether Sen no Rikyū ultimately became the victim of intrigues, that is, whether he was compelled to commit suicide after rumors had surfaced that the tea master had tried to poison his superior, is deliberately left unanswered in the novel. Thus Inoue's interpretation of Sen no Rikyū's violent end may also be seen as the perfect completion of a life planned and designed down to the last detail in the spirit of the way of tea.

Sen no Rikyū's achievement was to develop a culture of humility and at the same time a highly subtle cult of beauty in the gesamtkunstwerk that is the tea ceremony. This stood in a deliberate contrast to the opulence of courtly Japan during the Heian era (794-1185) practiced by the nobility at court and the Buddhist clerics of the time.

Suddenly, people discovered the charm in the absence of color, in asymmetry, in imperfection, in all that is incidental. The central tenet of this aesthetic principle is *wabi*, a term that is difficult to render in another language and denotes the beauty of all that is transitory, dark, melancholy and sparse. The Buddhist idea of vanitas, of the finiteness and inevitable mortality of human existence plays a key role. As early as 250 years prior to Rikyū, the monk Yoshida Kenkō commented in the "Tsurezuregusa" (translated as "Essays in Idleness" by Donald Keene[8] and quoted at the beginning of this contribution) that:
"To my knowledge a house is no more than a temporary shelter for a period of time; what a joy it is, however, to find one with harmonious proportions and an agreeable atmosphere. [...] A house [...] appeals to us if it is of an unpretentious beauty — a grove of trees with an indefinably old-fashioned aspect; [...]. A house that has been laboriously perfected by an army of craftsmen [...] is an ugly sight and entirely depressing."[9]

In this context it is important to emphasize that a teahouse should exude the transitory beauty that is alluded to in the previous paragraph even in the selection of the building materials. These are materials that can age and will eventually disintegrate into dust. It is interesting to note that the teahouse is referred to as *sō'an* or "grass hut" in Japan; in other words: a reed-covered shelter that provides protection from wind and the elements for the wanderer. Anyone who has looked at East Asian landscape paintings is familiar with this motif — in these images it is often the only trace of human civilization in a vast expanse of

[7] Op. cit., p. 124.
[8] In East Asia, grass (Japanese *kusa*) is a widely used metaphor for the transitoriness of life.
[9] Essays in Idleness (see ftn. 1), p. 10.

Sö'an ("grass hut"), Yamagata
Design: Toshihiko Suzuki, 2003
Shell (p. 82), tearoom with *nijiriguchi*,
the low entrance opening for guests
and interior view of tearoom
Sö'an („Grashütte"), Yamagata
Entwurf: Toshihiko Suzuki, 2003
Außenhaut (S. 82), Teeraum im
Inneren mit *nijiriguchi*, dem nied-
rigen Zugang für die Gäste sowie
Innenansicht des Teeraums

Nach der Besichtigung der Gegenstände wurde ein Mahl serviert, wobei es aufgrund der großen Zahl der Gäste zu Gedränge kam. [...] Inmitten des ganzen Trubels war der Taikō die auffälligste Erscheinung."[6]

Die Ambivalenz, mit der Sen no Rikyū und selbst der skrupellose Militärherr Hideyoshi diesem Pomp begegneten, wird wenige Zeilen später deutlich, wenn es heißt: „Es ist natürlich nur eine Vermutung, aber ich glaube, er ließ Hideyoshi noch am selben Tag zu einer schlichten und strengen Zeremonie in der zwei *tatami* großen Teeklause Yamazatoan antreten, die dieser eigens für Meister Rikyū errichtet hatte. Auf seine Weise war der Taikō durchaus ein hervorragender Kenner der Teezeremonie und wusste die entspannte Stimmung der Teeklausen Yamazatoan und Myōkian weit besser zu schätzen als viele andere."[7]

Diese Wendung zeigt zum einen die Janusköpfigkeit der Persönlichkeit Hideyoshis, der als Politiker die Teezeremonie als Machtdemonstration einsetzte, sie im Privaten jedoch ganz im Sinne des Meisters Sen no Rikyū als meditativen Akt betrachtete. Zugleich zeigt diese Passage, welche Macht der Teemeister tatsächlich über den mächtigsten Mann im Staat hatte. Ob Sen no Rikyū letztlich das Opfer von Intrigen wurde, sein Tod also erzwungener Selbstmord war, nachdem Gerüchte aufgetaucht waren, dass der Teemeister seinen Herrn vergiften wollte, lässt der Roman bewusst im Ungewissen. So mag in Inoues Interpretation von Sen no Rikyūs gewaltsamem Ende auch als Vollendung eines ganz und gar durchgeplanten Lebensentwurfs im Geist des Teewegs interpretiert werden.

Sen no Rikyūs Leistung war es, im Gesamtkunstwerk der Teezeremonie eine Kultur der Bescheidenheit und zugleich einen höchst subtilen Kult der Schönheit entwickelt zu haben. Diese bildete einen bewussten Gegenpol zur Prachtentfaltung des höfischen Japan der Heian-Zeit (794–1185), wie sie Hofadel und buddhistischer Klerus in jener Epoche pflegten. Plötzlich entdeckte man den Reiz des Farblosen, der Asymmetrie, des Unvollkommenen, des Beiläufigen. Der zentrale Begriff für dieses ästhetische Prinzip ist *wabi*, ein kaum übersetzbarer Terminus, der eine Schönheit des Vergänglichen, des Düsteren, Melancholischen und des Kärglichen meint. Der buddhistische Gedanke der Vanitas, der Endlichkeit, der Todgeweihtheit der menschlichen Existenz, ist hier von zentraler Bedeutung. Schon 250 Jahre vor Rikyū stellte der Mönch Yoshida Kenkō in dem am Anfang bereits zitierten „Tsurezuregusa" (wörtlich „Gras[8] der Langeweile", von Donald Keene übersetzt als „Essays in Idleness") fest:

„Ein Haus ist, soweit ich weiß, nur eine Behausung auf Zeit; aber was für eine Freude ist es, eines mit harmonischen Proportionen und einer angenehmen Atmosphäre zu finden. [...] Ein Haus [...] spricht uns an, wenn es von unprätentiöser Schönheit ist – ein Hain von Bäumen mit einem undefinierbar altertümlichen Antlitz; [...]. Ein Haus, das Heerscharen von Handwerkern mit großer Mühe aufpoliert haben, [...] ist hässlich anzusehen und vollkommen deprimierend."[9]

Es ist in diesem Zusammenhang wichtig zu betonen, dass ein Teehaus schon in der Wahl der Materialien, aus denen es gebaut ist, den hier skizzierten Aspekt der vergänglichen Schönheit zum Ausdruck bringen

[6] Inoue Yasushi: Der Tod des Teemeisters. Übersetzung: Ursula Gräfe. Frankfurt 2007 (jap. Original erschienen 1981), hier S. 123. Inoue hat diesen Roman, der als sein künstlerisches Vermächtnis gilt, auf der Grundlage des Erfahrungsberichts eines Schülers von Sen no Rikyū, Honkakubō, abgefasst.
[7] A.a.O., S. 124.
[8] Gras (jap. *kusa*) ist eine in Ostasien weit verbreitete Metapher für Vergänglichkeit.
[9] Essays in Idleness (wie Anm. 1), S. 10.

mountains, water and clouds. Lightweight, ephemeral materials are therefore the basis for teahouse architecture — Kengo Kuma, who feels a great kinship with this idea, speaks of breathing architecture in the context of his synthetic teahouse for the park of the Museum of Applied Arts. On another occasion, the architect expresses his overall skepticism of concrete as the universal building material of modernism. He emphasizes in this context how important it was for him to have grown up in a traditional Japanese wooden house.[10]

In teahouse architecture, stone is only used for stepping stones on the path to the teahouse and in the form of a water basin for hand washing at the low entrance to the house. All other components consist of timber beams, in part in their natural form, tree trunks that are simply polished or shellacked, of adobe walls, paper windows, wooden sliding doors and straw as roof covering. The modest dimensions of the hut are also important as a reflection of humility and awe in the face of the grandeur of nature and the immeasurable scale of the cosmos. As in all traditional Japanese architecture, the basic unit is based on the roughly mattress-sized *tatami* mat. In Yasushi Inoue's previously cited novel, Sen no Rikyū's student Honkakubō describes the tearoom in his monastic retreat with a floor space of only 1.5 *tatami* as "barely large enough for myself on my own."[11] This is undoubtedly the absolute minimum. Yet most tearooms are no larger than 4.5 *tatami*. Kengo Kuma's structure with a floor area of nine mats is extraordinary in scale. However, it is important to note that this floor space accommodates both the tearoom as such and the preparation

room, hidden behind a specially constructed screen.

Yet the architecture of the teahouse is no more than the setting for an art form that truly speaks to all the senses. In addition to the house itself and the surrounding garden, especially landscaped for this purpose, the tea ceremony also incorporates the art of flower arranging (*ikebana*), ceramics, calligraphy and painting, even the olfactory sense and of course the sense of taste are stimulated in a special way. With regard to the synaesthetic experience we have described, the second most important term aside from *wabi* is *suki* and it plays a decisive role. It refers to a special form of artistic enthusiasm, an aesthetic adventure that deliberately overthrows long-established habits of perception. In this manner the tea aficionado is constantly in search of extraordinary objects that can be integrated into the tea ritual. These may be rare collectibles such as a tea bowl from ancient China. On the other hand, I have witnessed a young Japanese tea mistress, who is also a film expert, place an image of John Cage at the center of a tea ceremony.[12] With unexpected items such as these, the tea ceremony gives rise to a moment of surprise, an aesthetic widening of the horizon so to speak. Above all, however, there is an ever present element of dynamism, just as the tea ceremony as such must always be understood as a performance. The act of serving and drinking tea only achieves its full potential through the movement in the space.

Interestingly *sō'an* ("grass hut") is complemented by another common word used to denote teahouse: *sukiya* (composed of the aforementioned *suki* and *ya* ["house"]

---

[10] Cf. Kengo Kuma: A Return to Materials. In: Luigi Alini: Kengo Kuma. Works and Projects. Milano: Electa, 2005, pp. 15 ff.

[11] The Death of the Tea Master (see ftn. 6), p. 13.

[12] On February 1, 1998, Yumi Machiguchi performed the fourth and final installment of a "hand-performance" based on the four seasons at Frankfurt's Museum of Applied Arts; "New River," a watercolor by John Cage from 1988 was the centerpiece of this performance.

Makoto Aida (born 1965): Portable Folding
Tea Ceremony Room, 2002
(Exhibition "Makoto Aida. Akira Yamaguchi,"
Tōkyō: Ueno no Mori Museum, 2007)
This is one of the most radical interpretations
of employing contemporary materials in teahouse architecture. The object can also be
understood as a satirical commentary on the
concept of the teahouse as a "grass hut"

Makoto Aida (geb. 1965): Portable Folding
Tea Ceremony Room, 2002
(Ausstellung „Makoto Aida. Akira Yamaguchi",
Tōkyō: Ueno no Mori Museum, 2007)
Dies ist eine der radikalsten Formen des
Umgangs mit zeitgenössischen Materialien
in der Teehausarchitektur. Das Objekt mag
auch als Persiflage auf das Konzept des
Teehauses als schlichte „Grashütte" zu ver-
stehen sein

sollte. Es geht um Materialien, die altern
können und letztlich zu Staub zerfallen.
Bezeichnenderweise wird das Teehaus in
Japan als sō'an („Grashütte") bezeichnet.
Es ist also ein riedgedeckter Unterstand,
der einem Wanderer Schutz vor Wind und
Wetter bietet. Jedem, der schon einmal ost-
asiatische Landschaftsmalerei betrachtet
hat, ist dieses Motiv bekannt – hier ist es
nicht selten die einzige Spur der menschlichen
Zivilisation in den unermesslichen Weiten
von Bergen, Wasser und Wolken. Leichte,
vergängliche Materialien bilden also die
Grundlage der Teehausarchitektur – Kengo
Kuma, der sich diesem Gedanken verbunden
fühlt, spricht im Zusammenhang mit
seinem Kunststoff-Teehaus für den Park
des Museums für Angewandte Kunst von
breathing architecture. An anderer Stelle
äußert der Architekt sein generelles Misstrauen
gegenüber Beton als dem universellen
Baustoff der Moderne. Er betont in diesem
Zusammenhang, wie wichtig es für ihn war,
dass er in einem traditionellen japanischen
Holzhaus aufgewachsen ist.[10]

Stein kommt in der Teehausarchitektur nur
in Form der Trittsteine auf dem Weg zur
Teehütte sowie in Gestalt eines Wasser-
beckens zum Händewaschen am niedrigen
Eingang des Hauses vor. Alles Übrige
besteht aus Holzbalken, teilweise in ihrer
natürlichen Wuchsform als Bäume, die
lediglich poliert bzw. lackiert sind, Lehmwänden,
Papierfenstern, hölzernen Schiebetüren und
Stroh zur Dachabdeckung. Wichtig sind
auch die bescheidenen Ausmaße der Hütte,
in denen sich Demut und Ehrfurcht vor der
Größe der Natur und der Unermesslichkeit
des Kosmos manifestieren. Das Grundmaß ist,
wie immer in der traditionellen japanischen

Architektur, die etwa bettmatratzengroße
tatami-Matte. Sen no Rikyūs Schüler
Honkakubō beschreibt in Yasushi Inoues
bereits zitiertem Roman den lediglich 1,5
tatami großen Teeraum in seiner Mönchsklause:
„gerade groß genug für mich allein".[11] Dies
ist zweifellos das absolute Minimum. Doch
die meisten Teeräume sind nicht größer als
4,5 tatami. Kengo Kumas Konstruktion mit
einer Größe von 9 Matten ist in ihren Aus-
maßen außergewöhnlich. Einschränkend ist
allerdings anzumerken, dass der eigentliche
Teeraum und, verborgen hinter einem speziell
konstruierten Stellschirm, der Anrichteraum
sich diese Fläche teilen.

Doch die Architektur des Teehauses bietet
nicht mehr als den Rahmen für eine tatsächlich alle Sinne ansprechende Kunstform.
Neben dem Haus selbst und dem ihn umgebenden, speziell für diesen Zweck angelegten
Garten kommen bei der Teezeremonie die
Kunst des Blumensteckens (ikebana), die
Keramik, Kalligrafie und Malerei zum Tragen,
ja selbst der Geruchssinn und selbstverständlich die Geschmacksnerven werden in
besonderer Weise angesprochen. Was die
hier skizzierte synästhetische Erfahrung
der Teekultur angeht, spielt der neben wabi
zweite wichtige Begriff suki eine entscheidende
Rolle. Er meint eine besondere Form des
künstlerischen Enthusiasmus, ein ästhetisches
Abenteuer, das bewusst althergebrachte
Wahrnehmungsgewohnheiten durchbricht.
So ist der Teemensch stets auf der Suche
nach außergewöhnlichen Gegenständen, die
in das Teeritual Eingang finden können.
Hierbei kann es sich um seltene Sammler-
stücke, zum Beispiel eine Teeschale aus
dem alten China, handeln. Ich habe es aber
auch schon erlebt, dass eine junge japanische

---

[10] Vgl. Kengo Kuma: A Return to Materials. In: Luigi Alini: Kengo Kuma. Works and Projects. Milano: Electa, 2005, S. 15 f.
[11] Der Tod des Teemeisters (vgl. Anm. 6), S. 13.

roughly translates as "site of fantasy." This helps us to understand why the interior of this site is limited to the simplest of objects, leaving the room in essence entirely bare. For it is the emptiness that allows the imagination and creativity to flower. The space is carefully prepared anew for each tea ceremony. One could say that the tea performance, which then follows, is a kind of mirror image of the dynamic processes of change to which nature — and the world as a whole — are constantly subjected. It is therefore entirely logical that the act of sharing the experience of imbibing tea should take place in a "grass hut," that is, in immediate proximity to open nature, which thereby becomes a part of the performance. As in most other fields of traditional Japanese art, conscious living with the seasons is part of the way of tea.

This specific becoming conscious of the processes of change in the world as a whole implies a special attention and awareness of the phenomenon of aging and wear-and-tear. All objects used in the context of the tea ceremony have a unique dignity of age. This allusion to wear-and-tear, to loving use over the course of many years, is understood as an aesthetic quality in the world of tea, expressed in the specially coined term *sabi* or the beauty found in the conditions of transitoriness. In the west, one would speak of patina. When rendered by a different Chinese character, *sabi* also means simply rust, corrosion. Sabi undoubtedly also has some relation to the aforementioned idea of *wabi*, that rough, sparse beauty which is closely linked to transitoriness, grief and death.

It is only too natural to pose the question how such a sensitive, melancholy cult of

beauty can survive in a world which, today more than ever, is characterized by noisy megacities, among them the 12-million capital of Tōkyō, the surroundings of which are home to roughly one third of Japan's entire population. This question was indeed already posed some one hundred years ago, when Japan rose to become Asia's first superpower in a brief time span of a few decades. In 1906, shortly after Japan's victory over Czarist Russia, Okakura Kakuzō (1862-1913) published "The Book of Tea"[13] in English and it quickly became one of the most popular books on Japan. Okakura's cultural theory, masterfully formulated in this work, influenced such diverse poets and thinkers as Martin Heidegger, Ezra Pound and Rabindranath Tagore.

At home in Japan, Okakura was instrumental in forging a culture of remembering "The Ideals of the East"[14] — which was also the title of his book published in 1903. Highly problematic in retrospect, this work undoubtedly proclaims Okakura as an intellectual trailblazer for Japan's extreme nationalism, whose fatal consequences for all of Asia and, last but not least, for Japan itself are universally known. In a wood-cut like manner, Japan's finely crafted culture is compared point by point against the western world in the age of imperialism, as powerful as it was decadent. The "Book of Tea," published three years later, appears somewhat more thoughtful and does indeed offer an excellent and easily understandable introduction to the art of the way of tea. It is interesting to note that it would be 1927 before this work was released in Okakura's mother tongue, at a time when the tea ceremony had come to be regarded as no more than an elegant pastime practiced by a small

[13] Okakura Kakuzō: The Book of Tea. New York: Putnam's, 1906.
[14] Okakura Kakuzō: The Ideals of the East. London: J. Murray, 1903.

Chazutsu, tea boxes of tin and copper. 1960 until 2007. Master Seiji Yagi for Kaikado, Kyōto. *Chazutsu*, Teedosen aus Zinn und Kupfer. 1960 bis 2007. Meister Seiji Yagi für Kaikado, Kyōto.

Teemeisterin, die zugleich Filmexpertin ist, ein Bild von John Cage in den Mittelpunkt einer Teezeremonie stellte.[12] Mit überraschenden Dingen wie diesen erwächst aus der Teezusammenkunft ein Augenblick der Überraschung, gewissermaßen eine ästhetische Horizonterweiterung. Vor allem schwingt hier stets ein Moment der Dynamik mit, wie überhaupt die Teezeremonie immer auch als Performance verstanden werden muss. Erst in der Bewegung im Raum gewinnt der Akt des Teeservierens und -trinkens seine volle Dimension.

Bezeichnenderweise ist neben *sō'an* („Grashütte") auch ein anderer Begriff für das Teehaus gebräuchlich: *sukiya*, zusammengesetzt aus dem eben vorgestellten Terminus *suki* und *ya* („Haus"), was also so viel bedeutet wie „Stätte der Fantasie". So wird auch begreiflich, weshalb sich die Einrichtung dieses Ortes auf die denkbar schlichtesten Dinge beschränkt und der Raum im Grunde vollkommen leer ist. Denn erst diese Leere bietet der Fantasie, der Kreativität eine Chance. Für jede Teezusammenkunft wird dieser Ort aufs Neue sorgsam vorbereitet. Die dann abgehaltene Tee-Performance ist gewissermaßen ein Spiegelbild der dynamischen Wandlungsprozesse, denen die Natur, das Weltganze, beständig unterworfen ist. Es ist somit auch nur konsequent, dass der Akt des gemeinsamen Teetrinkens in einer „Grashütte" stattfindet, also in nächster Nähe zur freien Natur, die so auch zu einem Bestandteil der Performance wird. Das bewusste Leben mit den Jahreszeiten ist ein selbstverständlicher Teil des Teeweges wie auch in den meisten anderen Bereichen traditioneller japanischer Kunst. Dieses spezifische Gewahrwerden gegenüber den Veränderungsprozessen des Weltganzen impliziert eine besondere Aufmerksamkeit gegenüber dem Phänomen der Alterung und der Abnutzung. Alle Dinge, die im Kontext der Teezeremonie zum Einsatz kommen, haben eine besondere Würde des Alters. Diese Anmutung von Abgenutztheit, von langjährigem, liebevollem Gebrauch, wird in der Welt des Tees als ästhetische Qualität begriffen – der Fachterminus hierfür ist *sabi*, was Schönheit unter den Bedingungen der Zeitlichkeit meint. Im Westen würde man von Patina sprechen. Mit einem anderen chinesischen Schriftzeichen geschrieben, bedeutet *sabi* auch schlicht Rost, Korrosion. Und zweifellos schwingt hier stets der oben schon skizzierte, ähnlich klingende Begriff *wabi* mit, also jene raue, kärgliche Schönheit, die sehr dicht an Vergänglichkeit, Trauer und Tod angenähert ist.

Es ist natürlich zu fragen, wie ein derart feinfühliger, wehmütiger Schönheitskult in einer Welt bestehen kann, die heute mehr denn je von lärmenden Megacitys geprägt ist, zu denen auf jeden Fall auch die 12-Millionen-Metropole Tōkyō gehört, in deren größerem Umfeld rund ein Drittel der japanischen Bevölkerung lebt. Diese Frage tat sich in der Tat bereits vor 100 Jahren auf, als Japan binnen weniger Jahrzehnte zur ersten Supermacht Asiens aufgestiegen war. Im Jahr 1906, kurz nach dem Sieg Japans über das zaristische Russland, brachte Okakura Kakuzō (1862–1913) „Das Buch vom Tee"[13] in englischer Sprache heraus, das schon bald zu einem der populärsten Bücher über Japan wurde. Okakuras in diesem Buch meisterhaft formulierte Kulturtheorie hatte Einfluss auf so unterschiedliche Dichter und Denker wie Martin Heidegger, Ezra Pound und Rabindranath Tagore.

---

[12] Am 1. Februar 1998 veranstaltete Yumi Machiguchi im Frankfurter Museum für Angewandte Kunst den vierten und letzten Teil einer auf die vier Jahreszeiten ausgerichteten „Hand-Performance", in deren Mittelpunkt die Arbeit „New River", ein Aquarell auf Papier von John Cage aus dem Jahr 1988, stand.
[13] Okakura Kakuzō: Das Buch vom Tee. Wiesbaden: Insel, 1954 (The Book of Tea. New York: Putnam's, 1906).

erudite elite in the face of the rapid rise of modernization that had swept over society as a whole.[15] Okakura may have been the first to discuss the way of tea as a specifically Japanese art form. In later years, the tea ceremony experienced a kind of renaissance even in modern Japan. The rich and powerful of the nation, especially the CEOs of large corporations, discovered collecting valuable tea paraphernalia as a new passion. A number of elegant museums in Japan, for example the Nezu Art Museum in Tōkyō, owe some of their finest exhibits to this new trend.[16] Incidentally, Kengo Kuma has been commissioned to create a new home for this renowned institution, scheduled to open in 2009.

The extraordinary popularity, which tea and the highly aesthetic Japanese tea culture currently enjoy around the world, is undoubtedly a welcome development in the interest of a peaceful evolution of human coexistence. Drinking tea, especially in the manner of the great Japanese tea masters, requires a culture based on contemplation and sensitive interaction with one's fellow beings and nature. Nevertheless one shouldn't turn into an unworldly romantic or a naive philantropist while following the way of tea; rather, one should always keep in mind that what is celebrated in the "grass hut" is an act of complete simplicity. Sen no Rikyū said it best:

The art of tea,
One should know,
Is no more
Than boiling water,
Preparing tea and drinking.[17]

[15] Cf. Hayashiya Tatsusaburō et al.: Japanese Art and the Tea Ceremony. New York/Tōkyō: Weatherhill/Heibonsha, 1974, p. 161.
[16] Founded in 1940, the Nezu Art Museum is named after Nezu Kaichirō, the director of the Tōbu Railway Company.
[17] The poem is taken from the Metsugo section of the Nanbōroku ("Memoirs of the Monk Nanbō"). Quoted from Toshihiko & Tōyō Izutsu: Die Theorie des Schönen in Japan. Beiträge zur klassischen japanischen Ästhetik. Cologne: DuMont 1988, p. 88.

Chasen, tea preparation brush,
since the 16th century
Chasen, Tee-Schaumbesen, seit
dem 16. Jahrhundert

In Japan selbst prägte er eine Kultur der Rückbesinnung auf die „Ideale des Ostens"[14] – dies der Titel eines 1903 erschienenen, aus heutiger Sicht höchst problematischen Werks, mit dem Okakura ohne Zweifel zu einem der geistigen Wegbereiter des japanischen Ultranationalismus wurde, dessen fatale Konsequenzen für ganz Asien und nicht zuletzt für Japan selbst allgemein bekannt sind. Holzschnittartig wird hier die feinsinnige Kultur Japans der ebenso mächtigen wie dekadenten westlichen Welt im Zeitalter des Imperialismus gegenübergestellt. Das drei Jahre später herausgekommene „Buch vom Tee" wirkt ein wenig nachdenklicher und bietet tatsächlich eine hervorragende und leicht verständliche Einführung in die Kunst des Teewegs. Interessanterweise erschien es erst 1927 in Okakuras Muttersprache, zu einer Zeit, als in Japan angesichts der die gesamte Gesellschaft erfassenden rasanten Modernisierung die Teezeremonie nur mehr als ein vornehmer Zeitvertreib für eine schmale Bildungselite betrachtet wurde.[15] Vermutlich war Okakura der Erste, der den Teeweg als eine spezifisch japanische Form von Kunst diskutierte. In der Folge erfuhr die Teezeremonie auch im modernen Japan neue Beachtung. Die Reichen und Mächtigen des Landes, vor allem die Direktoren der großen Wirtschaftsunternehmen, entdeckten das Sammeln von kostbarem Teegerät als neue

Leidenschaft. Etliche vornehme Museen Japans, etwa das Nezu Art Museum in Tōkyō, verdanken diesem neuen Trend einige ihrer qualitätvollsten Exponate.[16] Am Rande sei erwähnt, dass Kengo Kuma damit beauftragt wurde, für dieses renommierte Haus ein neues Gebäude zu entwickeln, das 2009 eröffnet werden soll.

Die außerordentliche Popularität, die der Tee als Getränk und die hochästhetische japanische Kultur des Tees derzeit weltweit genießen, ist zweifellos im Interesse einer friedlichen Fortentwicklung des menschlichen Zusammenlebens in jeder Hinsicht zu begrüßen. Tee zu trinken, zumal in der Nachfolge der großen Teemeister Japans, fördert eine Kultur des Nachdenkens und des sensiblen Umgangs mit den Mitmenschen und der Natur. Dennoch sollte man auf dem Teeweg nicht zum weltflüchtigen Romantiker oder verklärten Gutmenschen werden; vielmehr gilt es stets im Auge zu behalten, dass in der „Grashütte" ein ganz und gar schlichter Akt zelebriert wird. Sen no Rikyū hat dies treffend formuliert:

Die Kunst des Tees,
muss man wissen,
ist nichts anderes
als Wasser kochen,
Tee zubereiten und trinken.[17]

[14] Okakura Kakuzō: Die Ideale des Ostens. Leipzig: Insel, 1923 (The Ideals of the East. London: J. Murray, 1903).
[15] Vgl. Hayashiya Tatsusaburō u.a.: Japanese Art and the Tea Ceremony. New York/Tōkyō: Weatherhill/Heibonsha, 1974, S. 161.
[16] Das 1940 gegründete Nezu Art Museum geht auf Nezu Kaichirō zurück, den Direktor der Tōbu Railway Company.
[17] Das Gedicht erscheint im Abschnitt Metsugo der Schrift Nanbōroku („Niederschrift des Mönchs Nanbō"). Zit. nach Toshihiko & Tōyō Izutsu: Die Theorie des Schönen in Japan. Beiträge zur klassischen japanischen Ästhetik. Köln: DuMont 1988, S. 88.

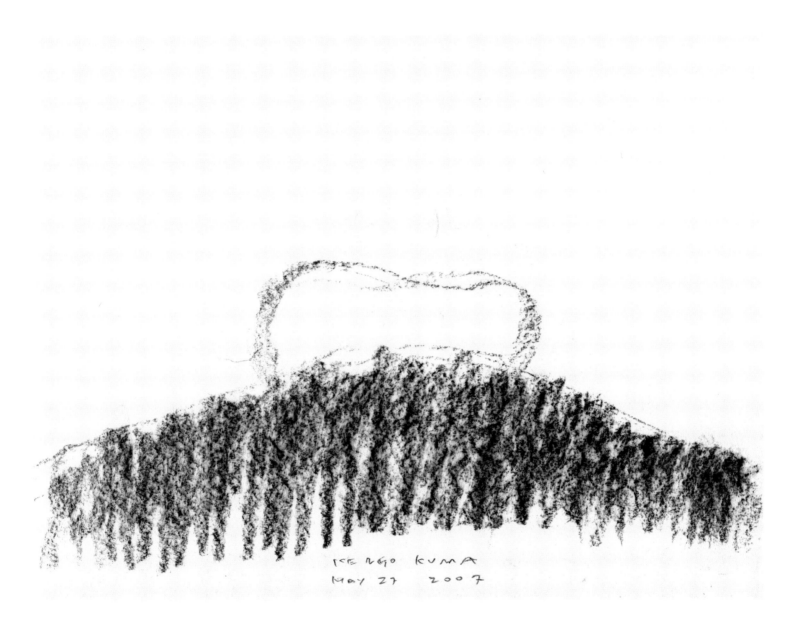

Kengo Kuma: logo sketch for the teahouse, May 2007
Kengo Kuma: Logo-Skizze für das Teehaus, Mai 2007

Kengo Kuma: computer-generated drawing for the
semitransparency of the teahouse, exterior, 2007
**Kengo Kuma: Computerzeichnung zur Semitransparenz
des Teehauses außen, 2007**

Kengo Kuma: computer-generated drawing for the
semi-transparency of the teahouse, interior, 2005
**Kengo Kuma: Computerzeichnung zur Semitransparenz
des Teehauses innen, 2005**

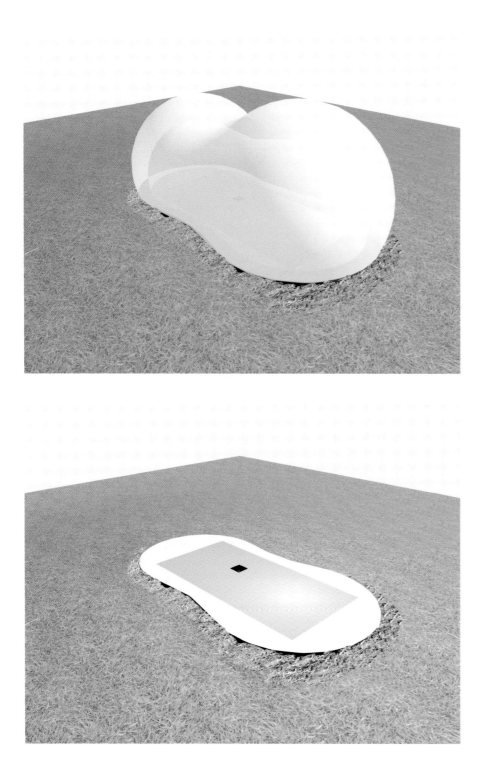

Computer-generated design of membrane shape,
February 2007
Computerplanung Membranform, Februar 2007

Computer-generated plan for foundation slab with *tatami*
sections, February 2007
**Computerplanung Bodenplatte mit *tatami*-Einteilung,
Februar 2007**

Kengo Kuma: computer-generated drawing of
semi-transparent teahouse at night, 2007
Kengo Kuma: Computerzeichnung des semitransparenten
Teehauses bei Nacht, 2007

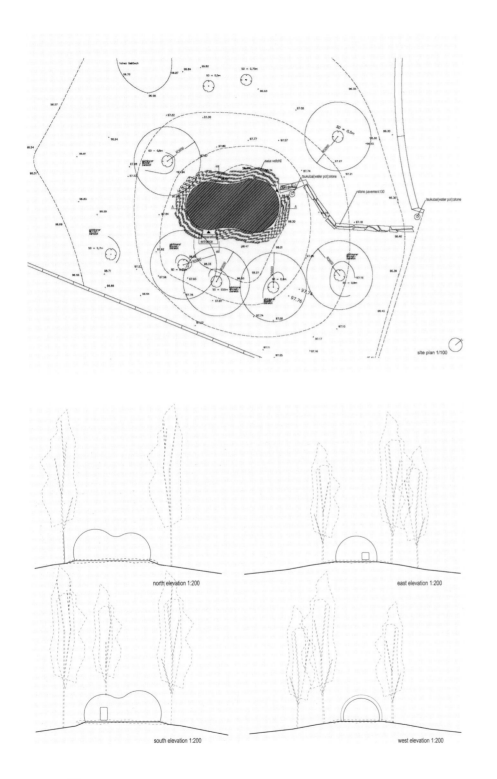

north elevation 1:200

east elevation 1:200

south elevation 1:200

west elevation 1:200

site plan 1/100

Site plan of teahouse, 2006
Lageplan des Teehauses, 2006

Teahouse elevations, 2006
Ansichten des Teehauses, 2006

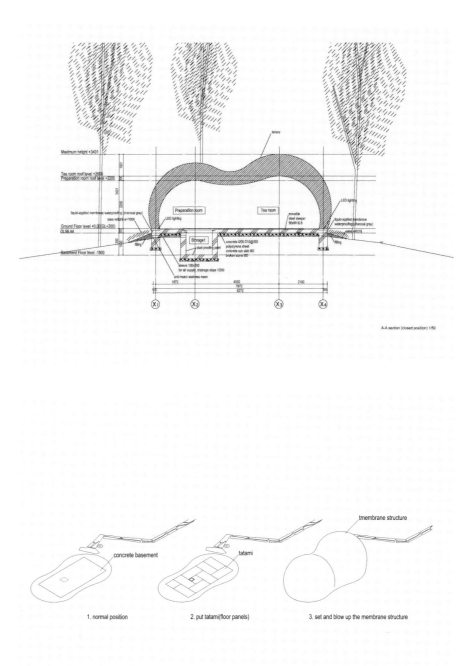

Maximum height +3401

tenara

Tea room roof level +2600
Preparation room roof level +2200

liquid-applied membrane waterproofing (charcoal gray)
suss veloch w=1000

Preparation room

Tea room

LED lighting

movable
steel sleeper
90x90 t2.6

LED lighting

liquid-applied membrane
waterproofing (charcoal gray)

Ground Floor level +0.00 (GL+200)
GL98.44

LED lighting

filling

Storage1

dust proofing paint

concrete t200 D10@200
polystyrene sheet
concrete sub slab t60
broken stone t80

filling

Basement Floor level -1800

sleeve 100x200
for air supply, drainage slope 1/200

anti-insect stainless mesh

1872   4000   2100
1972
8272

X₁   X₂   X₃   X₄

A-A section (closed position) 1/50

tmembrane structure

concrete basement

tatami

1. normal position

2. put tatami(floor panels)

3. set and blow up the membrane structure

A-A-section of teahouse with foundation and membrane,
as well as installation diagrams, January 2007
**A A Schnitt Teehaus mit Gründung und Membrane,
sowie Set up-Diagramme, Januar 2007**

95

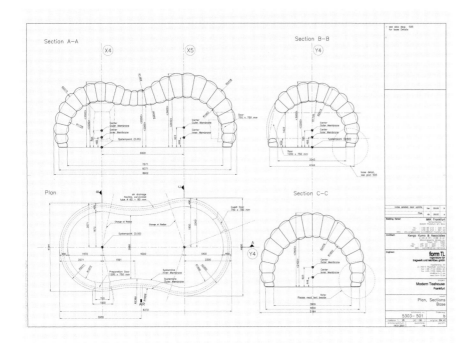

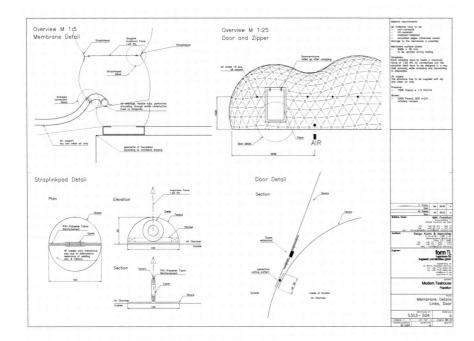

Working drawing for membrane, January 2007
Werkplanung Membrane, Januar 2007

Working drawing for membrane and delivery point,
January 2007
Werkplanung Membrane und Andienung, Januar 2007

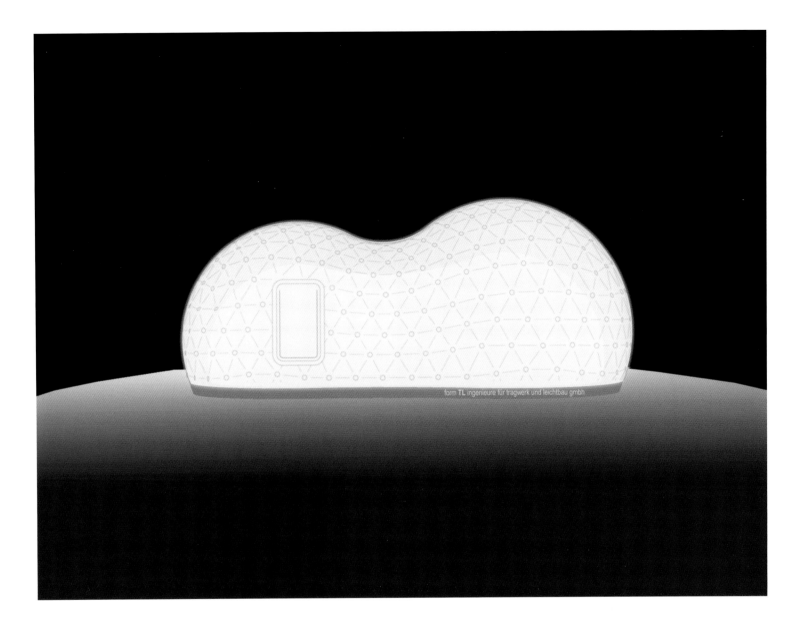

Geometric structure of membrane with welding
points for strap link cables
Geometrische Struktur der Membrane mit den
Anschweißpunkten der Koppelseile

Reinforcement of foundation slab
Bewehrung Bodenplatte

Application of finishing concrete layer
Auftrag der Feinbetonschicht

Formwork for foundation slab
Verschalung der Bodenplatte

Coated finishing concrete layer as base for the *tatami* mats
Gestrichene Feinbetonschicht als Untergrund für die *tatami*-
Matten

Foundation slab with LED channel
Bodenplatte mit LED-Rinne

Coated foundation slab with temporary weather shield
Gestrichene Bodenplatte mit temporärem Wetterschutz

Unfolding the membrane
Entfalten der Membrane

Positioning of membrane on foundation slab
Positionierung der Membrane auf der Bodenplatte

Membrane details, high performance zipper, filler neck

Details Membrane, Schwerlastreißverschluss, Einfüllstutzen

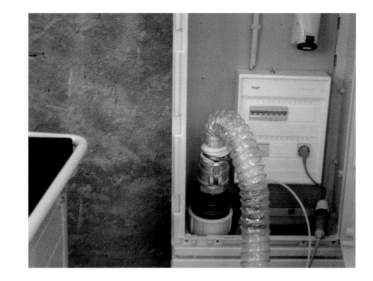

Details of filler neck for compressed air, compressor,
connection in foundation slab
Details Einfüllstutzen Pressluft, Kompressor, Anschluss
in der Bodenplatte

Injecting compressed air
Einblasen der Pressluft

Partially inflated membrane
Die teilaufgeblasene Membrane

Injecting compressed air
Einblasen der Pressluft

Nearly fully inflated membrane
Die fast vollständig aufgeblasene Membrane

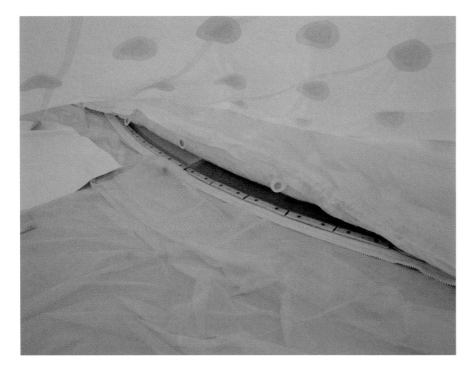

Connecting the membrane to the Keder profiles of the LED
channel with high performance zippers
Verbindung der Membrane mit den Kedernutprofilen der
LED-Rinne durch Schwerlastreißverschlüsse

High performance zipper
Schwerlastreißverschluss

Fully inflated teahouse

Das vollständig aufgeblasene Teehaus

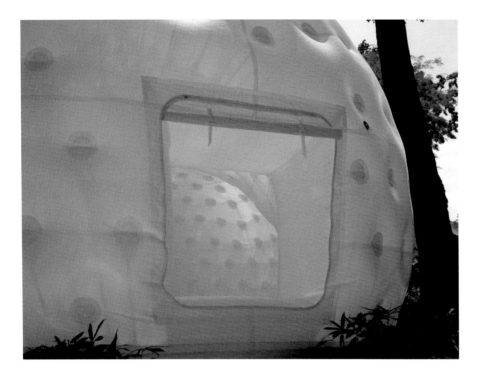

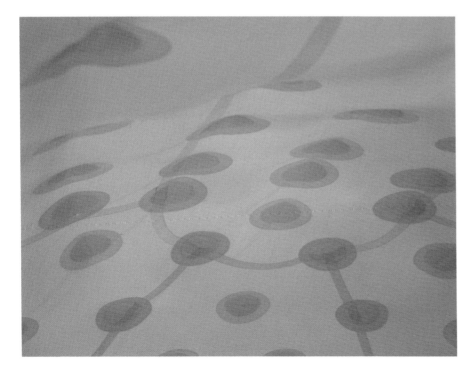

Entrance to guest room
Eingang zum Gastraum

Strap link cables of the double-shell membrane
in transmitted light
Koppelseile der zweischaligen Membrane im
Durchlicht

Teahouse in relation to the museum park

Das Teehaus im Dialog zum Museumspark

Tea path from restaurant patio to teahouse
Der Teeweg von der Restaurantterrasse zum Teehaus

Entrance to guest room with stone bowl for hand washing
Eingang zum Gastraum mit der Brunnenschale zum
Händewaschen

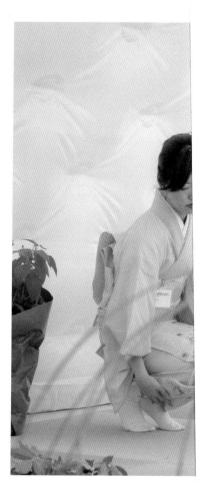

Preparation for tea ceremony

Vorbereitung der Teezeremonie

The sculptural membrane with welding points for strap link cables

Die skulpturale Membrane mit den Anschweißpunkten der Koppelseile

Tea ceremony assistants
Assistentinnen für die Teezeremonie

Inauguration of the teahouse on August 18, 2007
Eröffnung des Teehauses am 18. August 2007

Tea ceremony assistants
Assistentinnen für die Teezeremonie

Inauguration of the teahouse on August 18, 2007
Eröffnung des Teehauses am 18. August 2007

Preparation for tea ceremony
Vorbereitung der Teezeremonie

Tokonoma niche in the teahouse with more than
300-year-old bamboo vase
Tokonoma-Nische des Teehauses mit über
300 Jahre alter Bambusvase

View from guest room to screen behind which preparation
room is located
**Blick vom Gastraum zum Paravent, hinter dem sich der
Anrichteraum befindet**

The sculptural membrane with welding points for strap link cables

Die skulpturale Membrane mit den Anschweißpunkten der Koppelseile

Inauguration of the teahouse, Kengo Kuma

Eröffnung des Teehauses, Kengo Kuma

Tea ceremony with children
Teezeremonie mit Kindern

Tea ceremony performed by Japanese tea master
Sōshin Kimura
**Teezeremonie mit dem japanischen Teemeister
Sōshin Kimura**

Salutation rituals for the tea ceremony

Verbeugungsrituale der Teezeremonie

Kengo Kuma, Katinka Temme (Foreign Projects architect,
KKAA, Tōkyō), the tea master Sōshin Kimura, Takumi Saikawa
(Project architect, KKAA, Tōkyō)
Kengo Kuma, Katinka Temme (Foreign Projects architect,
KKAA, Tōkyō), der Teemeister Sōshin Kimura, Takumi Saikawa
(Project architect, KKAA, Tōkyō)

The teahouse at night with integrated LED illumination, seen from the East
Das Teehaus bei Nacht mit integrierter LED-Beleuchtung von Osten

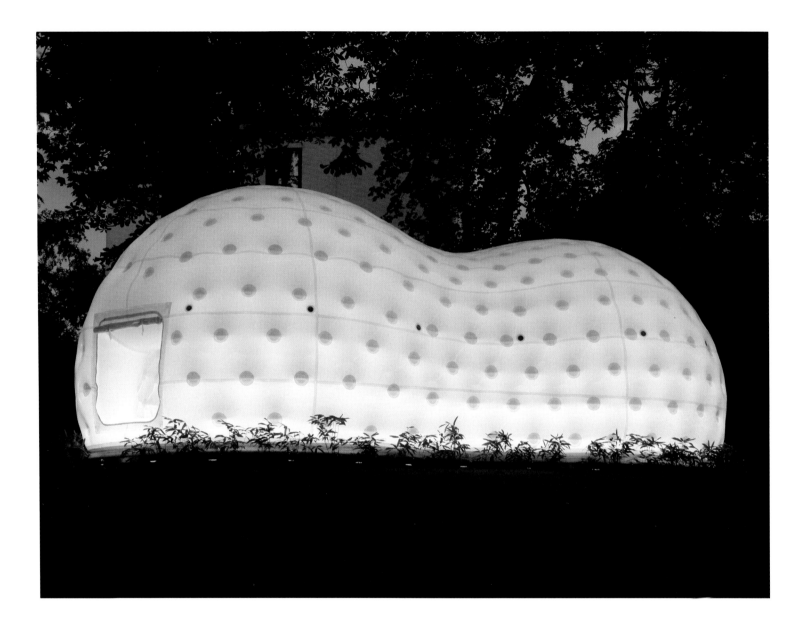

Teahouse at night, seen from the North

Das Teehaus bei Nacht von Norden

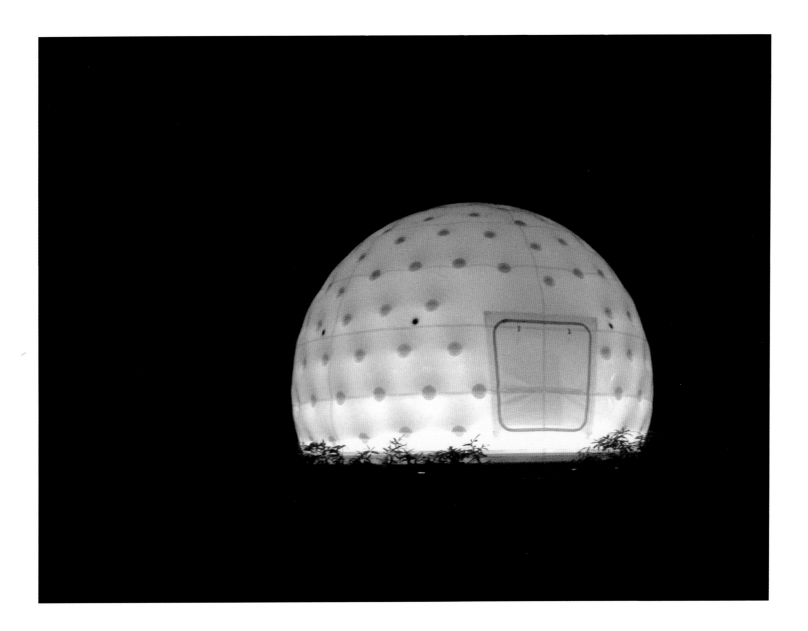

Teahouse from the East at night

Das Teehaus von Osten bei Nacht

West elevation of teahouse

Das Teehaus von Westen

Assistants to the tea master

Assistentinnen des Teemeisters

Preparation of tea ceremony (*chadō*)

Vorbereitung der Teezeremonie (*chadō*)

North elevation of teahouse

Das Teehaus von Norden

Kengo Kuma
1954 Born in Kanagawa Prefecture
1979 Completed the Master Course,
Department of Architecture, Graduate
School of Engineering, University of Tōkyō
1985-86 Visiting Scholar Graduate School,
Columbia University and Asian Cultural Council
1987 Established Spatial Design Studio
1990 Established Kengo Kuma & Associates
1998-99 Professor at the Faculty of
Environmental Information, Keiō University
2001 Professor at the Faculty of Science
and Technology, Keiō University

Takumi Saikawa
(born 1974 in Joetsū, Niigata Prefecture,
Japan)
Shibaura Institute of Technology, Tōkyō,
Japan
Graduated Master Course Keiō University,
Tōkyō, Japan
Established "MKT.A" in Rome, Italy
Massimiliano Fuksas Architects, Italy
At Kengo Kuma & Associates since 2004
Project Architect Nezu Museum, Tōkyō; Yien
East, Kyōto; Teahouse, Frankfurt

Katinka Temme
(born 1976 in Hilden, Germany)
University of Karlsruhe, Germany
Graduated Arizona State University, USA
with honors
Architect at Gerber Generalplaner
Architekten, Germany, and
Herzog & de Meuron, Switzerland
At Kengo Kuma & Associates since 2001
Project Architect for Great Bamboo Wall
(Phase II), Beijing; Z58 Shanghai, China;
Art Barn, Switzerland; House in the Alps;
Teahouse, Frankfurt

Kengo Kuma
1954 Geboren in der Präfektur Kanagawa
1979 Abschluss Masterkurs, Department of
Architecture, Graduate School of
Engineering, Universität Tōkyō
1985-86 Gaststipendiat Graduate School,
Columbia Universität und am Asiatischen
Kulturkonzil (Asian Cultural Council)
1987 Gründung Spatial Design Studio
1990 Gründung Kengo Kuma & Associates
1998-99 Professor an der Fakultät für
Environmental Information, Universität Keiō
2001 Professor an der Fakultät für Science
and Technology, Universität Keiō

Takumi Saikawa (geboren 1974 in Joetsū,
Präfektur Niigata, Japan)
Shibaura Institute of Technology, Tōkyō,
Japan
Abschluss Masterkurs Universität Keiō, Tōkyō,
Japan
Eigenes Büro „MKT.A" in Rom, Italien.
Architekt bei Massimiliano Fuksas
Architekten, Italien
Seit 2004 bei Kengo Kuma & Associates
Projektarchitekt für Nezu Museum, Tōkyō;
Yien East, Kyoto; Teehaus, Frankfurt

Katinka Temme
(geboren 1976 in Hilden, Deutschland)
Universität Karlsruhe
Abschluss Masterkurs Arizona State University,
USA, mit Auszeichnung
Architektin bei Gerber Generalplaner
Architekten, Deutschland;
Herzog & de Meuron, Schweiz
Seit 2001 bei Kengo Kuma & Associates
Projektarchitektin für die Great Bamboo Wall
(2. Phase), China; Z58 Shanghai, China; Art
Barn, Switzerland; House in the Alps;
Teehaus, Frankfurt

Works and Projects / Werke und Projekte

1988 Kyodō Grating (collaboration with Satoko Shinohara/Spatial Design Studio)/ Setagaya, Tōkyō, Japan
A Small Bathhouse in Izu (collaboration with Satoko Shinohara/Spatial Design Studio)/ Kamo-gun, Shizuoka, Japan

1989 GT-M (collaboration with CAD Institute for Planning)/Maebashi, Gunma, Japan

1992 RUSTIC/Shinjuku, Tōkyō, Japan
Maiton Resort (collaboration with Spatial Design Studio, Consultants of Technology)/ Maiton, Phuket, Thailand
Doric/Minato, Tōkyō, Japan
M2/Setagayaku, Tōkyō, Japan

1993 Kinjo Golf Club/Sojā, Okayama, Japan
Japan Museum (project planning)

1994 Kinjo Golf Club
Japan Museum (project planning)/Minatōku, Tōkyō, Japan
1994 MAN-JU/Sawara, Fukuoka, Japan
Yusuhara Visitor's Center/Yusuhara, Takaoka, Kōchi, Japan
Kirōsan Observatory/Yoshiumi, Ochi, Ehime, Japan
1994 Glass/Shadow/Tomioka, Gunma, Japan
Nōh Stage in the Forest/Tome, Miyagi, Japan
River/Filter/Tamakawa, Ishikawa, Fukuoka, Japan

1995 Water/Glass/Atami, Shizuoka, Japan
Space Design of Venice Biennale Japanese Pavilion/Venice, Italy
1995 Eco Particle (project planning)/ Mitakojima, Osaka, Japan
Reverse Theater/Chōfu, Tōkyō, Japan
Memorial Park (project planning)/Takasaki, Gunma, Japan

1996 Awaji S.A./Awaji, Hyōgo, Japan
EXPO 2005 Basic Conception (project planning)/ Seto, Aichi, Japan
Seaside Subcenter (project planning) /Minato, Tōkyō, Japan

1997 Wood/Slats/Hayama, Kanagawa, Japan
Kitakami Canal Museum/Ichinoseki, Miyagi, Japan
Super Street (project planning)

2000 Bato-machi Hiroshige Museum/Batō, Nasu, Tochigi, Japan
Takayanagi Community Center/Kashiwazaki, Niigata
Sakushin Gakuin University/Utsunomiya, Tochigi, Japan
Makuhari Housing Complex/Makuhari, Chiba, Japan
Nasu History Museum/Nasu, Tochigi, Japan
Stone Museum/Nasu, Tochigi, Japan

2001 Porous House – Kurakuen Project (project planning)
Institute of Disaster Prevention/Toride, Ibaraki, Japan
Parking Building Takasaki/Takasaki, Gunma, Japan
Sea/Filter/Onoda, Yamaguchi, Japan
Ginzan Bathhouse/Obanazawa, Yamagata, Japan
Bamboo House II – Kurakuen Project (project planning)
The Skin That Filters The River (urban project planning)

2002 Great (Bamboo) Wall/Beijing, China
PLASTIC HOUSE/Meguro, Japan
Adobe Museum for Wooden Buddha/ Shimonoseki, Yamaguchi, Japan
ADK Shōchiku Square/Chuō, Tōkyō, Japan

2003 Housing Exhibition Center/
Horai Onsen Bathhouse/Izu, Shizuoka, Japan
Forest/Floor/Karuizawa, Nagano, Japan
Soba Restaurant at Togakushi
Shine/Nagano, Nagano, Japan
Baiso Buddhist Temple/Minato, Tōkyō, Japan
JR Shibuya Station Renovation
Project/Shibuya, Tōkyō, Japan
One Omotesandō/Minato, Tōkyō, Japan
Great (BAMBOO) WALL — Phase 2/Beijing,
China
Shizuoka Expo Gate Building/Shizuoka, Japan

2004 Waketokuyama/Minato, Tōkyō, Japan
Shinonome Apartment Building/Koto, Tōkyō,
Japan
The "Food and Agriculture"
Museum/Setagaya, Tōkyō, Japan
Murai Masanari Art Museum/Setagaya,
Tōkyō, Japan
NTT Aoyama Building Renovation
Project/Minato, Tōkyō, Japan
LVMH Osaka/Chuo, Osaka, Japan
COCON Karasuma/Shimogyo, Kyōto, Japan

2005 Fukusaki Hanging Garden/Osaka, Japan
Nagasaki Prefectural Art Museum (collabora-
tion with Nihon Sekkei) Nagasaki, Japan
Bus Stop in Finland/Finland
KxK (Hara Museum of Contemporary Art,
Shinagawaku, Tōkyō)
Banraisha (collaboration with Taisei Corporation)
/Minato, Tōkyō, Japan
The Scape/Shibuya, Tōkyō, Japan
Lotus House/Eastern Japan

2006 Y-Hutte/Eastern Japan
Takanezawa Plaza/Shelter/Tochigi, Japan
Hoshinosato Annex/Kudamatsu, Yamaguchi,
Tōkyō

Ginzan Onsen Fujiya/Obanazawa, Yamagata,
Japan
Z58/Shanghai, China
Yusuhara Town Hall/Yusuhara, Kochi, Japan
Tōkyō Midtown Project D North Wing (collab-
oration with Nikken Kensetsu)/Minato, Tōkyō,
Japan
Asahi Broad Casting Corporation (upcoming
project) (collaboration with NTT Facilities)
/Osaka, Japan
Suntory Museum (collaboration with Nikken
Kensetsu)/Minato, Tōkyō, Japan
Tobata C Block Project (collaboration with
Takenaka Corporation)/Fukuoka, Japan
Dellis Cay Spa Resort (upcoming project)/
Cays of the Turks and Caicos Island
Suzhou Dwelling Project (upcoming project)/
Suzhou, China
23rd St. James Street (upcoming
project)/London, UK
Tenerife Housing Project (upcoming project)
Kenny Heights Museum (upcoming proj-
ect)/KL, Malaysia
Art Barn (upcoming project)
House in the Alps (upcoming project)
Modern Tea House Project in Frankfurt,
Germany
New Sunlitun Project-N1 Boutique Hotel
(upcoming project)/Beijing, China
Spiritual Center of Chengdu (upcoming
project)/Chengdu, China
Chengdu Library (upcoming project)/
Chengdu, China
Besancon City of Arts and Culture Architecture
(up-coming project)/Besancon, France
Complex of Government Buildings related to
the area of the "Eiffel Hall"-Western Railway
Station of Budapest (Budapest, Hungary)
(collaboration with Peter Janesch and Team)
Budapest, Hungary

Illustration Credits/Bildnachweis

Aato de sōrō. Aida Makoto, Yamaguchi Akira,
Tōkyō 2007: p. 84, 85

Abendroth, Uta; Phillips, Karin Beate et al.
(Eds.): das designbuch. Augsburg 1999:
p. 38 bottom.

Baacke, Rolf-Peter; Brandes, Uta u. a.
(Hrsg.): Design als Gegenstand: p. 39 top.

Ban, Shigeru. Projects in Process to Japanese
Pavilion, EXPO 2000, Hannover, Tōkyō 1999:
pp. 28 bottom, 29 top.

Bannwarth, Marie, Frankfurt:
pp. 22, 29, 98 top, 98 bottom, 99 top &
bottom, 100 top, 100 bottom, 101 top, 101
bottom, 102, 103, 104, 105, 106, 107, 110,
114 bottom, 115 116 top, 117, 122, 125

Bier, Michael: Asien: Straße, Haus – Eine
typologische Sammlung asiatischer
Wohnformen, Stuttgart 1990: pp. 26, 27

Coop Himmelblau. Architektur ist jetzt.
1968-1983, Stuttgart 1983: p. 33

Dettmar, Uwe, Frankfurt:
front cover, pp. 108, 109, 112, 116 bottom,
118, 119, 120, 121

Festo AG, Esslingen 1999:
p. 36 bottom, p. 37 top, 38 center.

Fischer, Volker, Frankfurt:
pp. 37 bottom, 38 top, 39 bottom,
40 top & center.

FormTL, Radolfzell:
pp. 66, 67, 68, 69, 70, 71, 72, 73, 74, 75
top, 96 top, 96 bottom, 97

Foscarini Srl (Hrsg.): Lux. Transparenza.
Transparency, Marcon, Italy 2007:
pp. 34 center, 35 bottom, 36 center,
41 bottom, 42 top, 42 center.

Freeman, Michael: New Zen. The tea-
ceremony room in modern japanese
architecture, London 2007:
pp. 80, 81, 82, 83 top, 83 bottom.

Futagawa, Yukio (Hrsg.): Kengo Kuma
(GA Architect 19) Tōkyō 2005:
pp. 24, 25 top

Gablowski, Birgit, Frankfurt:
pp.113 left,123, 124

Hayashitya, Tatsusaburō u. a.: Japanese Arts
and the Tea Ceremony, Tōkyō 1980:
pp. 9, 11, 13, 15, 78 top, 78 bottom, 79

http://www.creatableinflatables.com: p. 41 top

http://www.inflatablechurch.com:
p. 37 center

Katachi Form, Cat. Frankfurt 2007:
pp. 87, 89

Katō, Shūichi: Geheimnis Japan, Köln 1992;
pp.17 top, 17 bottom, 77

Kengo Kuma Architects Asp., Tōkyō:
pp. 10, 12, 14, 16, 18, 19, 21, 47, 48, 49,
50, 51, 52, 53, 54, 55, 65, 90, 91 top, 91
bottom, 92 top, 92 bottom, 93, 94 top, 94
bottom, 95

Klotz, Heinrich (Hrsg.): Haus-Rucker-Co.
1967 – 1983, Braunschweig, 1984:
pp. 32, 34 top, 35 center.

Roboter für Teezeremonie

Roboter üben den Umgang mit Flüssigkeiten. KEY

Tomomasa Sato, Tōkyō University: robot for tea ceremony, 2007
Tomomasa Sato, Universität Tōkyō: Roboter für Teezeremonie, 2007

"... they even wash up the dishes"[1]
„...und spülen können sie auch."[1]

---

[1] See "Roboter für Teezeremonie", in: Neue Zürcher Zeitung 9/03/2007.